EDUCATION AND LIVING

First published 1917
This edition published by Lector House in 2024

ISBN: 978-93-6138-085-3

Lector House LLP
Registered Office: H. No. 96, Block C, Tomar Colony,
Burari, Delhi – 110084, India
info@lectorhouse.com
www.lectorhouse.com

EDUCATION AND LIVING

RANDOLPH SILLIMAN BOURNE

2024

LECTOR HOUSE LLP

EDUCATION AND LIVING

BY

RANDOLPH SILLIMAN BOURNE

Author of "Youth and Life," "The Gary Schools"

PREFACE

These papers, reprinted with slight additions from the pages of the "New Republic," through the courtesy of the editors, do not pretend to be anything more than glimpses and paraphrases of new tendencies in the American school and college. The public school is the most interesting and the most hopeful of our American social enterprises during these days of sluggishness for us and dreary horror for the rest of the world. It is becoming one of the few rational and one of the few democratic things we have, and science and hope are laying a foundation upon which a really self-conscious society could build almost anything it chose. The school fascinates me because there is almost no sociological, administrative or psychological truth that cannot be drawn out of its manifold life. It is the laboratory for human nature, and the only one that is simple enough to study with any prospect of quick enlightenment. Experiment in education has come to stay, and this means that we have it in our hands to approach ever more closely our ideal of education as living. We can make the school ever more and more nearly that child-community life towards which our best endeavor points.

The point-of-view of these papers will be recognized as the product of an enthusiasm for the educational philosophy of John Dewey. But what is a good philosophy for except to paraphrase? The discovery of truisms means merely that my enthusiasms are being communicated to an unappreciative reader. Certainly the most recent educational sensation indicates that there are still crowds of professional educators and parents to whom such ideas are not truisms. To see education, not as a preparation for life or as a process segregated from other activities, but as identical with living, takes more imagination than most teachers have yet acquired. If the school is a place where children live intensively and expressively, it will be a place where they will learn. The ideal educational system would continue with the adult all through his or her active life, sharpening skill, interpreting experience, providing intellectual tools with which to express and enjoy. Just as education and play should be scarcely separable for the little child, so education and work should be scarcely separable for the adult. By closing off the school and boxing up learning we have really smothered education. We are only just beginning to revive. We have first to make over the school into a real child-community, filled with activities which stimulate the child and focus his interest towards some constructive work, and then we have to teach the teacher how to expose the child to the various activities and guide his interest so that it will be purposeful. The school can thus become a sifter where children unconsciously as they live along from day to day are choosing the ways in which they can best serve both themselves and their community as workers and citizens in the great scheme.

The papers on the Gary schools are reprinted not because I wish to exploit the system or its superintendent, but because of the usefulness of a concrete example to hang wandering theory to. The schools of Mr. Wirt's conception, in spite of many inadequacies of realization, still seem to me the happiest framework I have yet found in the American public school for the fulfillment of the new educational ideals. No one can deny that in the actual schools much of the old unconsciousness and regimentation still stick their unwelcome head through, but my somewhat naïve impressions do reflect, I am sure, a spirit which is there, and a possibility that is very near for the American community to catch. To praise one thing, however, is not to damn everything else, and it would be false to pretend that almost every city in our country has not latent within its system the embryo of the modern school. Some are simply more conscious than others. Some actually envisage education as living.

CONTENTS

EDUCATION AND LIVING

I

EDUCATION AND LIVING

What is the current broadening of the public school—the bringing in of gymnasiums and pools, shops and gardens, dramatics and organized play—but a new effort to realize the school as more a life and less an institution? Are we not getting a little restless over the resemblance of our schools to penitentiaries, reformatories, orphan asylums, rather than to free and joyous communities? A school system whose object was little more than to abolish illiteracy and prepare the more fortunate for college was bound to fall an easy prey to the mechanical organizer. Education in this country has been one-sidedly professionalized. The machinery was developed before the moving ideals were worked out. Professional educators have worked too much for a logical system rather than for an experimental adjustment to the life needs of individual children. We have achieved a democratic education in the sense that common schooling is practically within the reach of every one. But a democratic education in the sense of giving equal opportunities to each child of finding in the school that life and training which he peculiarly needs, has still to be generally worked for. The problem of American education is now to transform an institution into a life.

Let us not deny the value of that emphasis on administration. The slow progress from the diffuse district school to the well organized state system represents the welding of a powerful instrument for a future democracy to use. Centralized and efficient administration is indispensable for insuring educational benefits to all. But there is a danger that we shall create capable administrators faster than we create imaginative educators. It is so easy to forget that this tightening of the machinery is only in order that the product may be finer and richer. Unless it does so result in more creative life it will be a detriment rather than a good. For it is too easy to make the running of the machine, the juggling with schedules and promotions and curricula and courses and credits, the end. To institutionalize a social function is always the line of least resistance.

We are becoming used to the impressive schoolhouses that tower over the unkempt and fragile houses of our American towns. The school already overshadows the church. If this means that the school is the most important place in the community, then it is a hopeful sign. But if its slightly forbidding bulk means simply that there is another institution to put people through a uniform process, or indeed through any kind of process, then we are no further along. The educators of the last generation, whether from false ideas of democracy or from administrative convenience or necessity, imposed deadly uniformities of subject matter and method on the children in the schools. They assumed that a uniform process would give uniform results. But children are infinitely varied in temperament and capacity and interests. So the uniform process gave the most wildly heterogeneous results. And the present unrest arises from our amazed dissatisfaction that so admirable and long-continued a public-school education should have left the masses of children so little stimulated and trained.

The pseudo-science of education under which most of us were brought up assumed that children were empty vessels to be filled by knowledge. Teachers and parents still feel that to cut down an arithmetic hour to forty-five minutes is to deprive the child of a fourth of his education. But children are not empty vessels, nor are they automatic machines which can be wound up and set running on a track by the teacher. They are pushing wills and desires and curiosities. They are living, growing things, and they need nothing so much as a place where they can grow. They live as wholes far more than older people do, and they cannot be made to become minds and minds alone for four or five hours a day—that is, without stultification. The school forgets that we are only accidentally intellectual, that our other impulses are far more imperious. Because a teacher can secure outward order, it does not mean that she has harmonized the child's personality. She has not the least clue to the riot or apathy or delusion that may be going on inside him. She may easily become a drill-sergeant, but she must not think that she has thereby become an educational scientist.

To become that she will have to think of the school as a place where children spend their time living not as artificially segregated minds but as human things. She would have to judge their activities in terms of an interesting life. And that involves good health, play, sport, constructive work, talk, questioning, exercise, friendship, personal expression, as well as reading and learning. A place where children really lived would be a place that gave opportunities for all these activities to just the extent that children were individually capable of expressing themselves. Children want to be busy together, they want to try their hand at tools and materials, they want to find out what older people do and watch them at it. They have to flounder about and have all sorts of experiences before they touch their spring of interest and face their real direction. All their education is really acquired in the same random way that the baby learns to control his movements and respond to his environment. No matter how the school tries to organize their learning, and feed it to them in graduated doses, this way of trial and error is really the one by which they will learn. You have no way of guaranteeing that they will learn what you think you are teaching them. What you can do is to put them in a controlled environment where they will most frequently strike the electric contact of curiosity and response, and get experiences that thrill with meaning for them.

Life in its lowest terms is a matter of passing the time. It would be well if educators would more often remember this. If they did, would they not examine more carefully the life which they provide for growing youth? College and high school life is reasonably antiseptic, it is not oppressive, it is not particularly arbitrary or shabby. But compared abstractly with what might be a good life, given the interests and outlook and needed training of youth, would it not seem a little sorry? Is it not a travesty, except for the few, on a really stimulating and creative way of spending time? Suppose educators seriously measured their schools by this standard of the good life. Suppose we really tried to carry out the principle that the secret of life is to pass time worthily.

Most of this current educational interest is another stab at the age-long problem of making education synonymous with living. We are rediscovering the fact that we learn only as we desire, as we seek to understand or as we are busy. We are trying to make the school a place where children cannot escape doing these things. We see now that education has grown up in this country in a separate institutional compartment, jealously apart from the rest of the community life. It has developed its own technique, its own professional spirit. Its outlines are cold and logical. It is far the best ordered of our institutions. Its morale is the nearest thing we have to compulsory military service. There is something remote and antiseptic about even our best schools. They contrast strangely with the color and confusion of the rest of our American life. The bare class-rooms, the stiff seats, the austere absence of beauty, suggest a hospital where painful if necessary intellectual operations are going on. Additions of gymnasiums and shops and studios to such a school will do little to set the current of life flowing again. The whole school must be loosened up, the stiff forms made flexible, children thought of as individuals and not as "classes." Thus new activities must be woven into a genuine child-community life. These things must be the contacts with experience that waken and focus children's interests. They must be opportunities for spontaneous living.

The school constantly encroaches on the home. It provides play and work opportunities that even well-to-do homes cannot provide. It must take over too the free and comradely atmosphere of the homes and the streets where children play. Let teachers face the fact that they cannot teach masses of children anything with the assurance that they will really assimilate it. What they can do is to fill the school with all kinds of typical experiences, and see that children are exposed to them. They can see that children have a chance to dabble in them, touch tools and growing things, read books, draw, swim, play and sing. Let the teacher cleverly supervise and coördinate, see that the children's interests are drawn out, and that what they do contributes toward their growth. In the last analysis, each child will have to educate himself up to his capacity. He can only educate himself by living. The school will be the place where he lives most worthily.

Our best American public schools are already in sight of such an ideal. Americans need more than anything to learn how to live. This is the first business of education.

II

THE SELF-CONSCIOUS SCHOOL

In the educational excitement of to-day we scarcely realize how far the modern school is passing out of that era when the program for work and study was carefully constructed with a view to the child's "preparation for life." Educators saw the world as divided into two radically different classes, adults and school-children. The adults were functioning in a definite sphere, using a certain self-contained and common body of knowledge to do their work and make their way in the world. The children, on the other hand, were waiting like the little unborn souls in "The Blue Bird," to take their places in that active world. If their parents were using knowledge as a current intellectual coin with which experience could be bought and social exchange effected, the child who had any chance of succeeding as an adult would have to be put in possession of as much of this current coin as he could hold, quite regardless of his own enthusiasm for it or his own consciousness of what it was all about.

The free public school, therefore, became the place where children took into themselves such automatically usable knowledge as would be important for them in the remote future of their active adulthood. Since book-knowledge had acquired honorific distinction as the badge of a leisure class—and did not every democratic parent wish his child to "rise in the world"?—and since it was of all knowledge the most easily negotiable in the form of simple processes and facts, this type of knowledge became the stock of the school. Then at some time a not unintelligent attempt was supposedly made to compare this current stock of intellectual paper money with the specie circulating outside in the community at large, to see whether the school reserve was accurate and sufficient. This attention lapsed, however, and the curriculum became a closed system, handed down to the uncritical and unconscious child with the authority of prestige and the sanctions of school discipline.

In this unconscious school, knowledge was presented to us not as acquaintance with things but with "subjects." Text-books were given us holding the golden lore, and education became the slow nibbling away at their facts for six to twelve years. We came to think of ourselves as cupboards in which were laboriously stored bundles of knowledge. We knew dimly the shape of the articles and the distinction of the materials within. But we never expected to see the contents until we were grown, when we would joyfully open our packages and use them to the infinite glory of our worldly success and happiness. But it was a slow child who did not begin to suspect, long before his shelves were full, that most of his adult friends had lost no time, when their schooldays were over, in locking their cupboards and leaving their bundles to the dust and worms.

The fine technique of the unconscious school as worked out by educators in normal schools and teachers' colleges in the last forty years can be read in any current school survey. Here the coincidence of work and study with the child's interests is accidental. Indeed, many parents and teachers are still opposed to making too large a part of the curriculum appeal to the child's ephemeral interests. Discipline is still thought of not as willed skill, which it is, but as the ability to do painful things. A world where children do joyfully and well what interests them, instead of what is "good" for them (because unpleasant), still excites the envious mistrust of an older generation.

Yet the transformation from the unconscious school to the self-conscious school is the very kernel of the present educational excitement. The new schools which arouse enthusiasm are those in which the child is learning what has meaning to him as a child. He no longer does things because it is the "teacher's way." That old perverted honor of the teacher never to admit that she is wrong lest the child's confidence be disturbed and he become conscious and critical of the methods and materials of his education, is breaking down. We are learning that in the unconscious school the prizes go to the docile and unquestioning, not to those of initiative and skill. The school that keeps children in ignorance of what they are doing trains them for an uncritical life in society.

The discovery is not new that all the skill necessary to live an effective life in America to-day is not contained in a few readers, arithmetics, abridged histories and geographies, an elementary algebra and plane geometry, a Latin, Greek, or German grammar, with cullings from the works of Cæsar, Virgil, Xenophon, Cicero and Homer. When educators found that adult life overflowed these narrow limits, they introduced manual training, gymnastics, drawing and music; but the child became no more self-conscious, for these were merely additional "subjects." The radical discovery of to-day is that the adult world is not primarily engaged in turning information into power. The adult rarely has a historical or a geographical or an arithmetical thought unconnected with experience. What he does is to work very concretely at a myriad of occupations, intellectual and mechanical, concerned with making a living, bringing up a family, dealing with people, casting a vote, reading newspapers. He has a great diversity of horizons, and the most effective people are those who react most intelligently to their experience as a whole. Power and information increase together, not one at a time. The effective adult is a self-conscious personality. The only school which can be a genuine preparation for life is a self-conscious school. The child must learn to live in the same kind of world that his elders live in. The school must be the community in which his child-life develops. His play and work must be, first of all, interesting activity.

Fortunately the modern movement to make the school self-conscious has begun at the bottom. The four earlier years of the public school as taught by recently trained teachers are now generally filled, even in conservative city systems, with this new vivid consciousness. Dramatization, the learning of reading and writing and arithmetic through play, group-games and folk-dancing, gardening, constructive wood-working—all this is a sign of the growing self-consciousness of the school. In the more advanced schools, shop and science work, community excursions, illustrative drawing and design, fertilize the life of the older children. The most complete self-consciousness is realized in a school of the Wirt type, where all the varied activities are arranged to contribute to the upkeep or enrichment of the school plant and the school community. For the older children the expanding community becomes an extension of the school, and they learn the operation of the adult world by going out to see the institutions of their community and asking questions about them. In the self-conscious school the child's own curiosity sets the cue, and the school's work is to provide manifold opportunities for the satisfaction of that curiosity.

As this self-consciousness spreads up through the school system, we should get a new type of intelligence. Children will get a sense of means used for ends, and this sense is the most imperative discipline that we need. A revolutionary reorganization of the curriculum will be effected. Already unapplied mathematics and unrelated classics are passing. Yet those years which should most closely approximate in function and appreciation and in intellectual attitude the adult world remain unregenerated. Little seems to have been done to alter the old high school, still regarded principally as the gateway to the largely unconscious college. As a community of adolescent life, meeting sex-interests, new idealisms and new assertions, it is a failure. But as the older pedagogy fades out, and the younger children trained in the self-conscious school advance, we may expect a new orientation for the older years. Meanwhile our most valuable criterion for any school, public or private, city or rural, is, "How far towards self-consciousness, as expressed in the individual child and in the school community as a whole, has the school progressed?"

III

THE WASTED YEARS

Only one child out of fourteen in our school system ever reaches the high school; whatever education ninety per cent. of American children are to have they must acquire before they are fourteen years old. So elementary a fact as this, it would seem, should be at the background of every discussion and criticism of the public schools. Yet the most cursory inspection of the average city public school shows that its significance has only recently and very dimly been realized.

Indeed, as the average city public school is at present organized, there is every reason to believe that most of the children get practically all their education before their tenth year. Limited as this schooling is, they do not by any means get the full advantage of what is supposed to be given them. One can hardly come from a study of the everyday classroom work of the average city school without a conviction that there is disastrous intellectual leakage which has been strangely ignored by educators.

This leakage is not in the primary school and the high school. For the teaching of "the three R's" American normal schools and training colleges in recent years have worked out many admirable techniques, which seem to have been generally adopted. The younger generation of teachers is doing efficiently its work of giving the child a mastery of these essentials of civilized intercourse. The present primary school on its intellectual side is an efficient institution.

Similarly the high school has had a large amount of attention and skill lavished upon it. Its administrative peculiar problems have been studied and met. The best high schools have been made to approximate elementary colleges, with well-rounded courses of languages and sciences, of artistic, manual and physical work. For the highly selected group which reaches the high school it provides an excellent purely intellectual curriculum, both for higher study and for social orientation.

Between the primary school and the high school, however, there lies a desert waste of four years, the significance and possibilities of which seem to have been scarcely considered. They are the most urgent years of all, for in them the educator must give compensation to the children who are forced to leave school for the opportunities they are to miss. Yet these middle years of what used to be called the "grammar school" are now left not only unmotivated, but without any genuine educational function. Instead of being prophetic of the future they merely drag along the relics of the past. Some schools, it is true, have timidly brought down the beginning of high school studies into the lower grades, but in general the "grammar school" merely continues the interests of the primary school on substantially the same lines.

Fifteen years ago, when I went to school, there may have been some excuse for this system. Teachers may have been correct in their belief that it took the average child eight years to learn arithmetic, reading, writing, spelling, and a smattering of history and geography. To-day such an assumption is ridiculous. I have seen children in large classes in an ordinary city school system learn all the elements of "the three R's" in less than six months. The clear writing and accurate reading of little children in the first grade who have only been going to school for a few months is astonishing. It suggests that Mme. Montessori could scarcely have known of the excellence of elementary methods in this country when she urged her ideas as revolutionary. For these small children, as for the Montessori child, the competitive number-work, the writing from dictation, the oral reading, the spelling, seemed not drudgery but interesting activity. Astonishing, too, was the uniform excellence of the results.

Now it is little more than a truism to say that "the three R's" have not really been learned until they have become automatic, that reading, writing and arithmetic are not ends in themselves but merely the tools for work. To give command of the tools is the peculiar task of the primary school, and of the primary school only. If children can be given an acquaintance with "the three R's" in six months, it does not seem too much to expect them to acquire this automatic command in two or three years. It is incredible that the child should have to study eight years for this. Yet our elementary schools continue to assume that every child is thus mentally backward. In the higher grades we find the same subjects, formal reading lessons, formal penmanship lessons, formal arithmetic and spelling. But something has happened to these children. They are distinctly less interested, less interesting, and even less capable than the smaller children. It is depressing to realize that the elementary school has existed only to turn first-grade children into seventh-grade children, and to realize that most of the latter are nearing the end of their school-days and will pass out into the world with that intellectual listlessness and lack of command.

Let me suggest what has happened to these children. Formal work, the learning of any technique, is apt to be pleasurable as long as we can feel ourselves gradually acquiring a command over our instrument. But after we have acquired the technique and can rely upon our skill, there is no gain in continuing formal exercises. There is only gain in using our skill in real work, the work for which we have studied. If we have studied a language, we do not keep mulling over rules of grammar and vocabularies, but we try as soon as possible to read. The means now gives way to the end.

We can understand one cause for that situation of which employers complain when children come to them from the public schools unprepared in the very elements of education. In the bad memories, flimsy information, inability to write or spell or figure accurately, is found the very common indictment of the public school. The criticism is usually that the groundwork has been poor, that the children have not been trained in the fundamentals. If my thesis is correct, the groundwork has not been poor. Of recent years, it has, on the contrary, been unusually excellent and thorough. The leakage has come in the middle years, which have simply disintegrated the foundations. The school has sharpened the mind, and then, by providing only a repetition of formal work instead of practical opportunity for use of the acquired technique, has proceeded to dull it. Grammar has been studied, literature in a curiously desiccated fashion, political history, esoteric branches of arithmetic. Subjects like these have filled the time that might have been given to copious individual reading, to writing about what is read or experienced, to practical number-work in simple statistics or accounting. Time which might have been given, through use of pictures and newspapers, to the cultivation of an imaginative historical and geographical background, has gone into aimless memorizing, or into a glib use of words and phrases.

This situation is all the more preposterous because both the high school and college are full of studies that could be begun by the intelligent child as soon as a technical proficiency in "the three R's" was once obtained. What psychological law declares that before fourteen a human being is incapable of learning languages, the sciences, or even the sociological studies, but that after fourteen he is capable of learning all these things? As a matter of fact, most of these "higher" studies could be much more easily assimilated by the quick and curious mind of the younger child than by the older. And for the worker in any field, acquaintance with elementary science and the organization of society is so emphatically important that we cannot afford to let the vast majority of our citizens remain all their lives ignorant of their very terms. In the four years of the "grammar school" an intelligent interest could be awakened in these fields, and the main outlines grasped. This would not mean the addition of many new subjects to an already crowded curriculum. It would merely mean the dropping of "the three R's" back into their rightful place in the primary school. It would lighten rather than overburden the school. We should then have a fair division of labor and function between the schools, to the profit of both.

If there is one criticism of the public school system on its intellectual side that can justly be made general, it is this of the wasted years. The school has found itself in this paradoxical situation, that the more excellent became its primary methods the poorer became the product at the end of the system. This paradox is explained. Educators have simply failed to recognize that the sharper they made the elementary tools and the better the facilities of obtaining skill in their use, the more varied and immediate should be the work upon which the tools are to be exercised. They have failed to provide this work. They have left a leakage in public education which has almost defeated its own ends.

IV

PUZZLE-EDUCATION

How righteously indignant did our teachers use to be if we ever precociously objected to learning our mathematics and grammar in school on the ground that if we were going to be doctors or policemen we should never have any use when we grew up for that kind of knowledge! Were we not entirely too young to know at all what kind of knowledge we should need when we did grow up? Did not our teachers impress upon us that in some mysterious way all was grist that came to our intellectual mill? Did we wish to know merely what we could use in the daily grubbing of bread and butter? Was not the fine flower of education knowledge learned for its own sake? We could thus be assured, as we cubed our roots or diagrammed our sentences, that all this work was "training the mind," so that we could almost feel our mental muscles growing in strength and elasticity. We were too young to see it then, but some day we should be heartily grateful to our painstaking teachers. Some day, when we were successful men, we should come to appreciate the superior wisdom of this educational system against which our rational little wills so smolderingly rebelled.

In those days, would we not have given our young chances of promotion to see ranged up before the teacher a group of great grown men, the successful ones of the earth, to be put through the paces at which we kicked? Would it not have tickled us to see a class consisting of a state senator, a former lieutenant-governor, a manufacturer, a city official, a banker, a physician, a merchant, a lawyer, an editor, an engineer and a clergyman, trying to spell daguerreotype and paradigm, reconnaissance and erysipelas, guessing at the distance in degrees from Portugal to the Ural Mountains, locating the desert of Atacama and the Pamir Plateau, expressing 150° Cent. in terms of Fahrenheit, and finding the area of the base of a cylindrical 1 gal. can, 10 ins. high? If it was true that we should all find this knowledge useful some day, then it would be preëminently these men who were finding it useful now.

Let the news go forth to all the children of the land who are questioning the why and wherefore of what they are learning, that this thing has actually been done. The eleven men have been assembled in Springfield, Ill., and have had put to them these questions and others, all taken from the prescribed work of the local public schools. The class constituted one of those inquiries conducted with the deadly accuracy of a laboratory experiment by the Russell Sage Foundation. The results, it need hardly be said, were a complete demonstration of the intuition of our childish precocity. Not one of these eleven successful and intelligent gentlemen made so much as a passing mark in any subject. In the spelling-match the best record was six words out of ten, while one man, probably the editor, failed in every word. Only one of the pupils knew the capital of Montenegro, while neither he nor any of the others had the faintest reaction to Atacama or the Pamir Plateau, much less to the length of South America or the distance in degrees from Portugal to the Ural Mountains. Only one of the eleven could do the thermometer problem—he must have been in Paris once in January—and not one knew the specific gravity of alcohol when 2 liters weigh 1.58 kgms. As for the ten historical dates selected from ninety-one, the only date that as many as ten men knew was the attack on Sumter. Only one identified the date of the Mexican War, only one the surrender of Cornwallis.

It must have seemed very curious to the eleven to be presented with these questions, and then have the answers labeled "knowledge." How many of them drew the conclusion that our public schools were little more in the higher reaches than a glorified puzzle-party, where recitation is often more like a guessing of riddles, or trying to discover the answer from the teacher's tone, or the putting together of a puzzle-picture? Look at the average school text-book, with its neat and logical divisions, and see if you can't hear the dry crackle of the author's wit as he has worked out his ingenious riddles, pieced his cunning examples together, hunted the dictionary for words to spell, dissected his history, carved up a continent. The intellect feeds on syllogisms. Syllogisms are so much easier than appreciations. And really it is far easier to reason than to interpret. In the first you have merely to follow the beaten track, in the other you must break new paths and put the thing in your own new language. Yet this whirling around of the mental engine with the belting off is represented to us as a process of "training the mind." You might as well say that an athlete could best train his legs by standing on his head and waving them.

It is this scheme of puzzle-education which this Springfield inquiry—a characteristic flash, we take it, of American genius—has so tellingly shown up. And this riddle-curriculum tends to get worse instead of better as the science of text-book-making waxes and the machinery of scientific pedagogy accumulates. The avowed aim of teachers and training-colleges in recent years has been to discover pedagogical methods that would do the work regardless of the personality of the teacher. The riotous absurdities of this scheme are being revealed by such inquiries as these in Springfield. They suggest that the policy of having our next generation's mental attitudes, stock of information, personal qualities, and moral biases cultivated by unimaginative teachers whose intellectual capacity has been just sufficient to acquire a few routine methods of "conducting" a class and keeping order in a group of restless children, may have become antiquated. Our genuine education—that is, a familiarity with the world we live in—must wait until we get out of school. That may partly explain why most children are so anxious to leave.

Some people might find in this inquiry not so much an evidence of the inefficiency of our public schools as of how little intellectual baggage one needs to become successful and eminent in these United States. But this is in reality only to make a heavier indictment. It is still primarily the schools that have failed to make the intellectual baggage important to the minds of their pupils, that have left uncultivated their tastes and horizons. It is for this reason that our American intellectual background is so relatively thin.

V

LEARNING OUT OF SCHOOL

A recent correspondent of the "New Republic" columns declares that the real puzzle in education is as to content. She asks us to outline the facts we have found of value, so that she may be sure, as she confesses she is not now sure, what children should know when they leave school.

I search the memory of my nine years in the public schools, and wonder what I really learned there. I must have learned to read and write and spell and work sums, for I can do all those things now; but I came out with no connected sense of my country's history or that of any other, and if I had any geographical grasp, it came only from a certain abnormal delight I took in poring over maps by myself. Algebra, geometry and physics I recall to have passed before my attention. I was a very dutiful child, and it was my moral rather than my intellectual sense which enabled me to get "marks" in these subjects. I cannot say that they were "learned," in the sense of being woven into experience in any way. Latin rather appealed to me, chiefly because of its elegance of form, which I remember to have been curiously reinforced by the æsthetic format of the Collar and Daniell's text-book we used. Certain English classics appeared like dim ghosts on my horizon. At no time could I have given an intelligent account of the plot or argument of any of the books we read in Latin, Greek or German. The French and Italian which I picked up later I can read more easily than the German upon which I spent three school years. Imagined geographical wanderings, the disentangling of some verses of Vergil, certain neat algebraic solutions, are all of my "learning" that excited my interest or enthusiasm. Nine years seems an unconscionable time to spend learning these simple things.

I conclude that there is not much use teaching children things that they will not assimilate with their own curiosity, and connect with what they consider worth while in their world. In my own case this curiosity rarely worked in school. I cannot defend its algebraic and Vergilian workings except as springing from some embryo æsthetic sense. But the geographical enthusiasm is perfectly intelligible. It is connected with that intellectual education which I was pursuing parallel to my school work, and which merged with it only occasionally. This unofficial education, begun at a very early age, came through the medium of the newspaper. The "New York Tribune," lying freshly on our doorstep every morning, was gathered in like intellectual manna by my small and grateful self. It told me daily of a wide, fascinating and important world, and to it I reacted with never failing curiosity. On the political events, personalities, foreign wars, riots, strikes, plays, books, and music that streamed disorganizedly through its columns, no school subject threw any light except geography, which at least enabled me to place things on the map. History, which might have helped, was taught, not backwards, in the order that one's curiosity naturally approaches it, but forwards, so that at no time did we get within hailing distance of the present.

My real education, as I look back on it, consisted in making some sort of order out of this journalistic chaos. I got some help in the debates on current events which a radical superintendent introduced into our high school. I remember pulverizing, at the age of thirteen, my opponents in debate, with proofs that a ruthless dictatorship was the only form of government possible in the primitive state of Santo Domingo. Our household, however, was innocent of current discussion. The public library had not been born. I had to plot out this larger world by myself. Indeed, the grown-up people whom I sought seemed on the whole less familiar than I with the bearings of my curiosity. I cannot say that there was anything subtle or complicated or critical in my acceptance of the newspaper. It was all I could do to get the world mapped out, and become familiar with the names that I read. I remember following the Greco-Turkish War with a great deal of satisfaction, though the issues involved and the real military operations never meant anything at all. I got only the pleasant familiarity with this wider social world that one would get in meeting the same faces constantly in the street, without knowing the names of the people or speaking to them.

Whatever familiarity with the trend of events and the wider interests of men and women I had when I left school was obtained in this way. The school had been practically valueless in giving me the background of the intellectual world in which I was henceforth to live. My framework was bony enough and the content flimsy, but the outlines of my interests were there, and curiosity enough to keep me ceaselessly at filling in that content. Nothing has occurred since that time to show me, through various vicissitudes, that it was not the most useful I could have. That its foundations had to be laid outside the school seems to me a sheer waste of educational energy on the school's part.

Boldly then, and in true egocentric fashion, I say that the child when he leaves school ought to have the foundations of interest in the events and issues in which people generally are interested. These practically all come within the attention of the metropolitan newspaper. The child should be equipped to get some kind of intelligent reaction to what he reads there about political and sociological events and issues, personalities, art and literature. No one could accuse a curriculum based on the newspaper of being aristocratic, esoteric, or ultra-cultural. The newspaper is the one common intellectual food of all classes and types in the community. Many persons, it is true, may react only to certain specialized departments, and yet even into the most rudimentary journals filter most of these larger issues and events. To use this stock as clues and work out the historical, geographical, and cultural ramifications in the school curriculum would provide this broad familiarity with the world the child is to live in which I suggest. I would not make the horrifying proposal that the newspaper be used as a school text-book. I am too well aware of that cardinal tenet of current educational morality which banishes the newspaper entirely from the school. There is something rather symbolic about that tenet, by the way. But to use a sort of generalized newspaper as the nucleus and basis of a curriculum would be a different matter. It would be using the actual current life of society as the guiding thread of what the child is to know. As far as the purely intellectual content of the school is concerned, it would do what so many educators desire, connect the school with life.

This ideal may be incredible, but it is not necessarily impossible. Take the child at its lowest terms, as a troublesome little person whom its parents send to school to get it out of the way of the crowded home until it is old enough to go to work. Then take the present curriculum, a medley of equally emphasized cultural, scientific and manual studies. Now the child certainly should have a command of the three R's before he is ten years old. Suppose then we transfer the mathematical and scientific studies to a place subsidiary to the vocational and manual work that is being so rapidly developed. They would be taken up, that is, only as the theoretical basis for this practical work. This would leave four or five years for the study of the history, geography, literature, language, and civics, before the minimum age at which the child in the more advanced states is allowed to leave school. There seems to be no inherent reason why a great deal could not be done in that time to prepare this imaginative background for the world we live in.

If "cultivating the imagination" means anything it means ensuring that what one experiences in daily life will call up interesting and significant images and ideas. The public school sometimes attempts to cultivate a sort of literary and mythological imagination, but as for ensuring that those references to places, persons, books, political institutions, ideas, which occur in the papers and weekly journals, shall call up to the mind prompt, accurate, and stimulating images and meanings, it has been a dead failure. An exploration of the current imagination of the average person would be a curious and profitable enterprise for a psychologist to undertake. For the cultivation of this imagery, we are all left, as the child is left, to the chance provision of the contemporary news-provider, the illustrated paper and "Sunday magazine." Here is where we get our notions of things as they look and act.

Beyond all else the child should leave school with a wide and reliable imagination—not with facts or theories so much as pictures, sympathies, apprehensions, what we call "the feeling for the thing." Thus equipped, his curiosity will provide him with all the facts and theories he needs. The custom of teaching by subjects is as artificial and absurd as could be imagined. We do not think in terms of history or geography or language. If I read a foreign newspaper, all these are merged into one imaginative impression. We think in terms of situations, which have settings in time and place, and all sorts of fringes and implications. Unless the child is taught in this spirit, the isolated subjects will have no meaning. Without the imaginative background that fuses and vitalizes his studies, he will go out from school untaught and unknowing.

VI

IN A SCHOOLROOM

The other day I amused myself by slipping into a recitation at the suburban high school where I had once studied as a boy. The teacher let me sit, like one of the pupils, at an empty desk in the back of the room, and for an hour I had before my eyes the interesting drama of the American school as it unfolds itself day after day in how many thousands of classrooms throughout the land. I had gone primarily to study the teacher, but I soon found that the pupils, after they had forgotten my presence, demanded most of my attention.

Their attitude towards the teacher, a young man just out of college and amazingly conscientious and persevering, was that good-humored tolerance which has to take the place of enthusiastic interest in many of our American schools. They seemed to like the teacher and recognize fully his good intentions, but their attitude was a delightful one of all making the best of a bad bargain, and coöperating loyally with him in slowly putting the hour out of its agony. This good-natured acceptance of the inevitable, this perfunctory going through by its devotees of the ritual of education, was my first striking impression, and the key to the reflections that I began to weave.

As I sank down to my seat I felt all that queer sense of depression, still familiar after ten years, that sensation, in coming into the schoolroom, of suddenly passing into a helpless, impersonal world, where expression could be achieved and curiosity asserted only in the most formal and difficult way. And the class began immediately to divide itself for me, as I looked around it, into the artificially depressed like myself, commonly called the "good" children, and the artificially stimulated, commonly known as the "bad," and the envy and despair of every "good" child. For to these "bad" children, who are, of course, simply those with more self-assertion and initiative than the rest, all the careful network of discipline and order is simply a direct and irresistible challenge. I remembered the fearful awe with which I used to watch the exhaustless ingenuity of the "bad" boys of my class to disrupt the peacefully dragging recitation; and behold, I found myself watching intently, along with all the children in my immediate neighborhood, the patient activity of a boy who spent his entire hour in so completely sharpening a lead-pencil that there was nothing left at the end but the lead. Now what normal boy would do so silly a thing or who would look at him in real life? But here, in this artificial atmosphere, his action had a sort of symbolic quality; it was assertion against a stupid authority, a sort of blind resistance against the attempt of the schoolroom to impersonalize him. The most trivial incident assumed importance;

the chiming of the town-clock, the passing automobile, a slip of the tongue, a passing footstep in the hall, would polarize the wandering attention of the entire class like an electric shock. Indeed, a large part of the teacher's business seemed to be to demagnetize, by some little ingenious touch, his little flock into their original inert and static elements.

For the whole machinery of the classroom was dependent evidently upon this segregation. Here were these thirty children, all more or less acquainted, and so congenial and sympathetic that the slightest touch threw them all together into a solid mass of attention and feeling. Yet they were forced, in accordance with some principle of order, to sit at these stiff little desks, equidistantly apart, and prevented under penalty from communicating with each other. All the lines between them were supposed to be broken. Each existed for the teacher alone. In this incorrigibly social atmosphere, with all the personal influences playing around, they were supposed to be, not a network or a group, but a collection of things, in relation only with the teacher.

These children were spending the sunniest hours of their whole lives, five days a week, in preparing themselves, I assume by the acquisition of knowledge, to take their places in a modern world of industry, ideas and business. What institution, I asked myself, in this grown-up world bore resemblance to this so carefully segregated classroom? I smiled, indeed, when it occurred to me that the only possible thing I could think of was a State Legislature. Was not the teacher a sort of Speaker putting through the business of the session, enforcing a sublimated parliamentary order, forcing his members to address only the chair and avoid any but a formal recognition of their colleagues? How amused, I thought, would Socrates have been to come upon these thousands of little training-schools for incipient legislators! He might have recognized what admirably experienced and docile Congressmen such a discipline as this would make, if there were the least chance of any of these pupils ever reaching the House, but he might have wondered what earthly connection it had with the atmosphere and business of workshop and factory and office and store and home into which all these children would so obviously be going. He might almost have convinced himself that the business of adult American life was actually run according to the rules of parliamentary order, instead of on the plane of personal intercourse, of quick interchange of ideas, the understanding and the grasping of concrete social situations.

It is the merest platitude, of course, that those people succeed who can best manipulate personal intercourse, who can best express themselves, whose minds are most flexible and most responsive to others, and that those people would deserve to succeed in any form of society. But has there ever been devised a more ingenious enemy of personal intercourse than the modern classroom, catching, as it does, the child in his most impressionable years? The two great enemies of intercourse are bumptiousness and diffidence, and the classroom is perhaps the most successful instrument yet devised for cultivating both of them.

As I sat and watched these interesting children struggling with these enemies, I reflected that even with the best of people, thinking cannot be done without talking. For thinking is primarily a social faculty; it requires the stimulus of other minds to excite curiosity, to arouse some emotion. Even private thinking is only a conversation with one's self. Yet in the classroom the child is evidently expected to think without being able to talk. In such a rigid and silent atmosphere, how could any thinking be done, where there is no stimulus, no personal expression?

While these reflections were running through my head, the hour dragged to its close. As the bell rang for dismissal, a sort of thrill of rejuvenation ran through the building. The "good" children straightened up, threw off their depression and took back their self-respect, the "bad" sobered up, threw off their swollen egotism, and prepared to leave behind them their mischievousness in the room that had created it. Everything suddenly became human again. The brakes were off, and life, with all its fascinations of intrigue and amusement, was flowing once more. The school streamed away in personal and intensely interested little groups. The real world of business and stimulations and rebounds was thick again here.

If I had been a teacher and watched my children going away, arms around each other, all aglow with talk, I should have been very wistful for the injection of a little of that animation into the dull and halting lessons of the classroom. Was I a horrible "intellectual," to feel sorry that all this animation and verve of life should be perpetually poured out upon the ephemeral, while thinking is made as difficult as possible, and the expressive and intellectual child made to seem a sort of monstrous pariah?

Now I know all about the logic of the classroom, the economies of time, money, and management that have to be met. I recognize that in the cities the masses that come to the schools require some sort of rigid machinery for their governance. Hand-educated children have had to go the way of hand-made buttons. Children have had to be massed together into a schoolroom just as cotton looms have had to be massed together into a factory. The difficulty is that, unlike cotton looms, massed children make a social group, and that the mind and personality can only be developed by the freely inter-stimulating play of minds in a group. Is it not very curious that we spend so much time on the practice and methods of teaching, and never criticize the very framework itself? Call this thing that goes on in the modern schoolroom schooling, if you like. Only don't call it education.

VII

THE CULT OF THE BEST

A valuable inventory of our American ideals of taste and culture should result from the request of the American Federation of Arts that the Carnegie Foundation undertake an investigation of the teaching of art in this country. We have devoted much attention to importing æsthetic values and works of art from Europe, and to providing museums, libraries and art courses for the public. But we have scarcely asked ourselves what is to come of it all. A survey of what is being done "in the schools and colleges and universities as well as in the professional art schools of the country to promote the knowledge, appreciation and production of art in America" will be of little value, however, if it is to concern itself merely with discovering how many art schools and how many students there are; how many courses on art are given in the colleges, and the credits which each course counts towards the degree. What we need to know is the direction of the studies. We must not feel relieved in spirit if we find there is "enough," and correspondingly depressed if we find there is "not enough" being done for art in America. We must clear up our ideas as to what a genuine art education would be for the layman, and then ask whether the present emphases are the ones to produce it.

Artistic appreciation in this country has been understood chiefly as the acquiring of a familiarity with "good works of art," and with the historical fields of the different arts, rather than as the cultivating of spontaneous taste. The millionaire with his magnificent collections has only been doing objectively what the anxious college student is doing who takes courses in the history and appreciation of art, music or literature, or the women's clubs that follow standard manuals of criticism and patronize bureaus of university travel. Everywhere the emphasis is on acquisition. A great machinery for the extension of culture has grown up around us in the last generation, devoted to the collection, objectively or imaginatively, of masterpieces. The zealous friends of art in and out of the schools have been engaged in bringing before an ever-widening public a roster of the "best." Art education has been almost entirely a learning about what is "good." "Culture" has come to mean the jacking-up of one's appreciations a notch at a time until they have reached a certain standard level. To be cultured has meant to like masterpieces.

Art education has, in other words, become almost a branch of moral education. We are scarcely out of that period when it was a moral obligation upon every child to learn to play the piano. There is still a thoughtful striving after righteousness in our attendance at the opera. And this moral obligation is supported by quasi-ecclesiastical sanctions. Each art, as taught in our schools and colleges, has its truly formidable canon of the "best," and its insistent discrimination between the sanctified and the apocryphal scriptures. The teaching of English literature in the colleges is a pure example of this orthodoxy. Criticism and expression are neglected in favor of absorption and reverence of the classics. The student enters college on a ritual of examination in them. He remains only through his susceptibility to their influence. Examine what passes for cultural education in other fields, and you will find that it is historical, lexicographical, encyclopædic, and neither utilitarian nor æsthetic. It is prompted by the scholarly ideal rather than by an ideal of taste. The prize goes to those who can acquire the most of these goods. No one is challenged to spontaneous taste any more than the monk is asked to create his own dogmas.

To me this conception of culture is unpleasantly undemocratic. I am not denying the superlative beauty of what has come to be officially labeled "the best that has been thought and done in the world." But I do object to its being made the universal norm. For if you educate people in this way, you only really educate those whose tastes run to the classics. You leave the rest of the world floundering in a fog of cant, largely unconscious perhaps, trying sincerely to squeeze their appreciations through the needle's eye. You get as a result hypocrites or "lowbrows," with culture reserved only for a few. All the rest of us are left without guides, without encouragement, and tainted with original sin.

An education in art appreciation will be valueless if it does not devote itself to clarifying and integrating natural taste. The emphasis must be always on what you do like, not on what you ought to like. We have never had a real test of whether bad taste is positive or merely a lack of consciousness. We have never tried to discover strong spontaneous lines of diversified taste. To the tyranny of the "best" which Arnold's persuasive power imposed upon this most inquisitive, eager and rich American generation, can be laid, I think, our failure to develop the distinctive styles and indigenous art spirit which the soil should have brought forth abundantly. For as long as you humbly follow the best, you have no eyes for the vital. If you are using your energy to cajole your appreciations, you have none left for unforced æsthetic emotion. If your training has been to learn and appreciate the best that has been thought and done in the world, it has not been to discriminate between the significant and the irrelevant that the experience of every day is flinging up in your face. Civilized life is really one æsthetic challenge after another, and no training in appreciation of art is worth anything unless one has become able to react to forms and settings. The mere callousness with which we confront our ragbag city streets is evidence enough of the futility of the Arnold ideal. To have learned to appreciate a Mantegna and a Japanese print, and Dante and Debussy, and not to have learned nausea at Main street, means an art education which is not merely worthless but destructive.

I know that such complaints are met by the plea that the fight has been so hard in this country to get any art education at all that it is idle to talk of cultivating public taste until this battle is won. Mr. Edward Dickinson still pleads in a recent book the cause of music to the stony educationists of the land. Let us get a foothold in the colleges with our music courses, these defenders seem to say, and your taste will evolve from them. But the way to reach a goal is not to start off in the opposite direction, and my thesis is that education in the appreciation of art has been moving exactly in this wrong direction. Widespread artistic taste would have had a better chance to develop in this country if we had not been so much concerned with knowing what we ought to know and liking what we ought to like. The movement has caught those whose taste happened to coincide with the canons. It has perverted a much larger host who have tried to pretend that their taste coincided. And it has left untouched the joyous masses who might easily, as in other countries, have evolved a folk-culture if they had not been outlawed by this ideal.

The ideal still dominates, although it becomes every day more evident that its effect has been disastrous. A younger generation of architects has filled our cities with sepulchral neo-classicism and imitative débris of all the ages. We get its apotheosis in the fantasy of Washington, where French chateaux snuggle up close to colonial mansions, and the great lines of the city are slashed by cheap and tawdry blocks. All this has been done with the best will in the world, by men curious and skilful, well instructed in the "best" of all time. It has been a conscientious following of an ideal of beauty. We are just beginning to discover uneasily how false that ideal is. Art to most of us has come to mean painting instead of the decoration and design and social setting that would make significant our objective life. Our moral sense has made us mad for artistic "rightness." What we have got out of it is something much worse than imitation. It is worship.

This effort to follow the best, which even our revolutionists engage in, has the effect of either closing the appreciation to new styles or leaving it open to passing winds of fashion. That we are fashion-ridden is the direct result of an education which has made acquisition and not discrimination the motive. The cult of the best is harmless only if it has been superimposed on the broadest basis of personal discrimination, begun in earliest years. Let us admit that the appreciations of the Brahmins marvelously coincide with what Matthew Arnold has stamped as right. But perhaps for most of us there has not been the environment to produce that happy coincidence. Our education has forced us all to be self-made men in artistic appreciation. Our tastes suffer from hiatuses and crotchinesses and color-blindnesses because no effort has been made to integrate our sincere likes and dislikes and focus and sharpen our reactions. Until the present ideal is overthrown, we have no chance of getting a sincere and general public taste. We can have only the mechanics of art education. I do not mean that America has been unique in this. We have only been a little worse than other countries because we have been more conscientious.

VIII

EDUCATION IN TASTE

There is a naïvely systematic way of teaching artistic appreciation to the students of many of our city schools. To each class is allotted a famous painter. The class is then taken en masse to the art museum, and, under the guidance of one of the official show-women, confronted with the masterpieces of its proprietary genius. The children hear the dates of the painter's life, details of his career, the significance of his pictures, the particular beauties of his styles, and any other loose fragments of knowledge that may appeal to their guide. After they have been exposed long enough to the pictures to give confidence that appreciation has taken place in them, they are allowed to exchange painters with another class, and in rigid platoon proceed to appreciate their new idol in the same way. Presumably their appreciation finally flows over the entire museum, and they take their places among the cultivated of the land.

The other day in a New Jersey school I was shown some wall-paper designs that had just been made in a class of the youngest children. A simple figure had been given them with which to cover a sheet of paper in any pattern they chose. The thirty papers presented the most astonishing variety. They ranged from mere blotches to orderly and regular patterns. Some children had merely reproduced the figure in parallel lines across the paper. Others had alternated their lines and made a more pleasing scheme. Here was a living demonstration of the variety of artistic skill, but I was more interested in the appreciation. The teacher told me that she had pinned all the designs on the wall, and without any suggestion to the children had asked them to choose which they liked best. There had been a large consensus of liking for the alternate lines, the pattern which was obviously the most regular and the most pleasing.

In that museum system of class-painters who were to be duly "appreciated" I had a perfect example of the old unregenerate cult of the best. But my New Jersey school convinced me that these vestal virgins of the museums were guarding a decaying fane. The young teacher in the classroom had the beginnings of what would be a genuine education in taste. If that same critical and discriminating spirit could be carried forward with these littlest children all through their schooling, most of them would get a robust sense of values that would be spontaneous, that would never have to be cajoled, and that could not be threatened. Might not this process of refining taste be woven into our elementary education? Already we have its embryo in these kindergartens and lower grades. It is a question of emphasis, of making the teachers see that the constant challenge to taste is one of the most important functions of the school. Types of school such as the Play-

School make expression and selection the basis of their life. The most valuable feature of the Montessori school is the training of the senses, the quickening of response to sounds and colors and forms. Suppose a child were brought up from his earliest years in everyday contact with forms and colors, without its ever being hinted to him that some were "good" and others "bad." Suppose the child were urged to choose and to express his likes and dislikes, not giving his reasons but merely telling as he could what he saw or heard. Suppose this attempt were made through the course of his school life to clarify his appeals and repugnances, not by rationalizing them but by synthesizing them. Would not something like taste evolve out of it all?

Emphasis on what the pupil likes instead of what he ought to like would change the tone of school or college. The average mediocre student under our present regime gets an almost uncanny desire to do things "right." Since success in school depends on doing what the teacher thinks is right, education becomes on the child's part a technique of accurate guessing. Anyone who has spent much time in high schools knows how eagerly children will pounce on any official judgment concerning a book or person or picture or idea. The study of English classics in most schools becomes a festering bed of hypocrisy. And it is often the intrinsically amenable who are the most conscientious and who therefore most hopelessly overlay their own reactions with other people's judgments. The modern school recitation has degenerated into a skilful guessing on the part of the child of what the teacher "wants" him to say. And this is a symbol of the general attitude, in school and out, towards cultural things.

A laudable attempt has been made in the colleges to teach the student to think, but I wonder sometimes whether it has proceeded very far beyond encouraging him to find reasons for ideas and attitudes which he is persuaded he ought to have. For most college students it is already too late. Expression and discrimination are the last things which the primary and secondary schools have been emphasizing. The boy and girl come to college with no background of taste or selection, and the old docility, the old unconscious hypocrisy, must dog them all through their course. I would make a larger part of the process of thinking in school and college the discovery of what one likes and wants, the control and direction of desire. Almost the whole object of education should be to know what one truly and wholeheartedly likes and wants.

Yet the modern school is just the place where this critical, discriminating attitude has a chance of being cultivated. The secret of all the current tendencies towards the "school of to-morrow" is the increasing participation of the children in the work of their own school. The Wirt plan, where the children help the mechanics decorate the rooms, and dramatize their school-life in auditorium exercises, perhaps carries this coöperation farthest, but in numberless schools that have shopwork, gardens, dramatizations, etc., the same evolution is apparent. Now every touch of dramatic, artistic and literary expression made by the children in the school affords material for education in taste. Expression and criticism play into each other's hands. Any expression which passes without a reaction from some part of this little school public is expression wasted. If the child does not learn in the school to observe and reflect upon and react to the expressive life that flows around him in the school, he will never react intelligently to anything outside the school. His childish criticism will of course be as elementary as the expression is elementary. But the emphasis of teachers should be there. Taste must flow naturally and spontaneously out of the experiences of everyday life.

Such an effort in the education of taste has a much better chance of success than has our traditional guidance. To impose canons on a younger generation, to make students appreciate the best in the arts, we need hosts of teachers who are finely tuned to these appreciations themselves, teachers whose tastes naturally coincide with what has been consecrated by time, and who can communicate their admirations. Experience has proved that we shall never have those hosts of teachers. We should never have enough Matthew Arnolds to go round. What art education suffers from in this country is teachers who have only the mechanics of appreciation without the inner glow. And it is futile to expect that we shall ever have enough with the classic inner glow. In this new direction, however, the teacher need not be mentor, but guide and provocative. Never being called upon to impart judgments or appreciations to the student, what he requires most is not judgments and appreciations of his own but curiosity as to the student's reactions. He need only be saying constantly to the student, what do you like and how does it compare with something else that you like? He need provide only the paraphernalia of art, the materials and processes, for the student to do his own work. If the teacher is of sound original taste, he can give the student criticism and aid him in his analysis and comparison. If he is not, he is at least prevented from making the student's taste hypocritical.

If this attitude became general in our æsthetic education, it would not be long before results became noticeable. We should get a variety of tastes—some of them traditional, some of them strange and new, but most of them at least spontaneous, indigenous. At present we have no way of knowing whether any particular manifestation of public taste is conventional, fashion-induced, imitative, or sincerely felt. Much spontaneous taste might turn out to be traditional. The majority of children trained in discrimination might prove to be incipient Brahmins. On the other hand we might get strange and vigorous expressions like the contemporary architecture and sculpture of Germany. I am assuming that taste and creation will fertilize each other. For this fertilization we must have a liberation of taste from the sterile control of the "best." This does not mean that every person would become endowed with original taste, but that we should have a chance to find original taste out. We should have done all within human power to create public taste, as our present ideal does everything to prevent it. As a result we should have a chance of some kind of integrated culture. In each art we might find several very strongly marked directions of style and taste which should appeal to different people. It would then be the task of criticism not to choose between them but to discover their sincerity and significance. Style is a matter of right relations. Things have style when their parts make each other and the whole significant. Indigenous style is the only art that really means anything. Out of an education in taste will grow creative art as a flower from rich soil.

IX

UNIVERSAL SERVICE AND EDUCATION

The current agitation for preparedness has set hosts of Americans to thinking out for the first time what a real national strength and readiness would mean. We suddenly realize that if we are to defeat that militaristic trend which we loathe we shall have to offer some kind of action more stirring and more creative. The call now upon every citizen is to be not nebulously patriotic, but clear and lucid as to America's aims, so that our natural energy shall not be squandered and misused. There looms up as a crucial need that "moral equivalent for war" with which William James first roused our imaginations. It seems no longer so academic a proposal. Confronted with the crisis, we see that he analyzed the situation with consummate accuracy.

All around us we see a very genuine craving for unity of sentiment, for service, for some new national lift and broadening which shall keep us out of the uneasy pettiness into which the American conscience has threatened to fall. In our hearts we know that to crystallize this desire into a meaningless sentiment, or into a piling-up of armaments or a proscribing of alien cultures, would not satisfy us. We want action, but we do not want military action. Even the wildest patriots know that America would have to go through the most pernicious and revolutionary changes to accept the universal military service which they advocate. We wish to advance from where we stand. We begin to suspect that military service, flag-reverence, patriotic swagger, are too much the weary old deep-dug channels into which national feeling always runs and is lost. The flooding river fills again its archaic and forsaken paths. Our present confusion expresses the dilemma we find ourselves in, when our instincts impel us into courses that our intelligence tells us we ought not to follow.

Our American danger is not so much that we become militarists as that we grope along, fretting and harrying each other into a unity which is delusive, and expressing our "Americanism" in activities that are not creative. The best will in America at the present time seems to crave some kind of national service but it veers off from military service. Until we satisfy that craving, we shall run at half-power, and suffer all the dissatisfaction and self-despising that comes from repressed energy. The question which all are asking, in the varied and disguised forms, is: How can we all together serve America by really enhancing her life?

To more and more of us the clue has come through James's conception of a productive army of youth, warring against nature and not against men, finding in drudgery and toil and danger the values that war and preparation for war have given. Ten years ago such an army seemed Utopian. We had neither the desire nor the technique. It seemed a project not to be realized without a reorganization of our life so radical as to make the army itself unnecessary. To-day, however, a host of new attitudes seem to give us the raw material out of which such a national service could be created. We hear much of universal military service as "education." The Plattsburgs are sugar-coated as "civic-training camps," "schools for citizenship." Universal service no longer stands on its old ground of mere preparation for war. It is frankly trying to get itself recognized as an indispensable mode of education. The next pertinent step is evidently to ask why, if universal service is valuable because it is educational, it should not be constructed on a strict educational foundation.

James's proposal sounded Utopian because it would require an entirely new and colossal national organization to put it into action. Universal military service in this country would certainly mean such a task. But if our national service is to be educational, we already have the organization in existence. The rapidly consolidating public school systems in the states provide the machinery for such an organization. As the public schools become better places for children to spend their time in, we are growing less tolerant of the forms of schooling outside of the public system. The tendency is towards the inclusion of all children in the public school. And the progressive states are requiring schooling up to the full age of sixteen years. We are rapidly creating a public school system, effectively administered by the states, which gives us the one universally national compulsory service which we possess or are ever likely to consent to.

Education is the only form of "conscription" to which Americans have ever given consent. Compulsory military service would require decades of Napoleonic political evangelism to introduce. Compulsory education is universally accepted. For a national service which shall be educational you would have to convert nobody. The field is sown. No one denies the right of the state to conscript the child for education. But coupled with this assent is the insistence that the education shall be the freest, fullest and most stimulating that we know how to give. The current educational interest arises largely from the indignant demand that a state which takes all the children must meet the needs of every child. The very recent enthusiasm for "vocational education" means that we want a schooling that shall issue in capacity for fruitful occupation. A national educational service could give training for work at the same time that it gave opportunity for service.

It is only a national service of this kind that would really be universal. Military service is a sham universality. It omits the feminine half of the nation's youth. And of the masculine half it uses only the physically best. France is the only country where the actual levy on men for military service has approximated the number liable. But worst of all, military service irons out all differences of talent and ability. It does not even tap the resources it enlists. It makes out of an infinitely varied group a mere machine of uniform, obeying units. The personal qualities, the individual powers of the youth it trains, are of no relevance whatever. Men are valuable exactly to the degree that they crush out these differences.

A national service for education would not be a sham. It would actually enlist the coöperation of every youth and girl. It would aim at stimulation, not obedience. It would call out capacity and not submerge it. It would organize varied tasks adapted to the capacities and strengths of its young citizenry. It would be universal, but it would be compulsory only in the sense that it called every one to the service. The tasks would not be enforced drudgery, but work that enlisted the will and toned up the aspirations.

Such a national service would be the logical outgrowth of our public school system. Suppose the state said: All children shall remain in school till the age of sixteen years. Between the ages of sixteen and twenty-one they shall spend two years in national service. This service shall be organized and administered by the state educational administrations, but supervised and subsidized by the national government. The service would be performed as national service, but its work would be constructive and communal in its purposes and not military. Special military training could be given as a branch of this service to those who were best fitted for it. But defense would be but an incident in our constructive life, and not the sinew of our effort.

The tasks for such a national service would evidently be different from those contemplated by James. He thought of turning his army of youth into the drudgery of the world, where they might win in heroic toil and self-sacrifice the moral rewards which war had formerly given. But if our service is to be universal, it cannot be mere unskilled labor in mines and farms and forests. A large proportion of our youth would be disqualified. Furthermore, a service which made such frontal attack on industry would be bitterly resisted by those with whom its work competed. We are not prepared for a service which clashes too suddenly and harshly with the industrial system. What we need is a service which shall not so much do the old work of the world as create new demands and satisfy them. This national service could do the things which need to be done, but which are not now being done. It could have for its aim the improvement of the quality of our living. Our appalling slovenliness, the ignorance of great masses in city and country as to the elementary technique of daily life—this should be the enemy of the army of youth. I have a picture of a host of eager young missionaries swarming over the land, spreading the health knowledge, the knowledge of domestic science, of gardening, of tastefulness, that they have learned in school.

Such a service would provide apprentices for communal services in town and country, as many schools and colleges are already actually providing. Food inspection, factory inspection, organized relief, the care of dependents, playground service, nursing in hospitals—all this would be a field for such an educational service. On a larger scale, tree-planting, the care and repair of roads, work on conservation projects, the care of model farms, would be tasks for this army. As I was burning caterpillars' nests the other day in New Jersey and saw the trees sinister with gray webs, I thought of the destroying army of youth that should be invading the land clearing it of all insect pests. We might even come to the forcible rebuilding of the slovenly fences and outhouses which strew our landscape, and to an imposition of cleanness upon our American countryside. With an army of youth we could perform all those services of neatness and mercy and intelligence which our communities now know how to perform and mean to perform, but have not the weapons to wield.

The army could be organized in flying squadrons, so that its youth could travel widely and see and serve all kinds of men and communities. For its direction we would need that new type of teacher-engineer-community-worker that our best school systems are already producing. Scientific schools, schools of philanthropy, are turning out men and women who could step into their places as non-commissioned officers for such an army. The service could be entirely flexible. Boys and girls could learn the rudiments of their trade or profession in actual service with the army. Book studies could be carried on, and college learning could come to its own as the intellectual fertilizer of a wholesome and stimulating life. Athletics and sports would be an integral part of the two years' service. There would be long periods of camping in the national parks or upon ocean beaches. The Boy Scouts and Camp-Fire Girls already give the clue to such an enterprise.

If objection is made that this national educational service would fail to bring out the sterner qualities of heroism and self-sacrifice, and would not be a genuine moral equivalent for war, the answer is that the best kind of a moral equivalent is a moral sublimation. We want to turn the energies of youth away from their squandering in mere defense or mere drudgery. Our need is to learn how to live rather than die; to be teachers and creators, not engines of destruction; to be inventors and pioneers, not mere defenders. Our cities and isolated farms alike are mute witnesses that Americans have never learned how to live. Suppose we had a national service which was making a determined assault for the enhancement of living. Would its standards and discipline be less rigorous? Rather would the ingenuity and imagination have to be of the finest.

Some such conception of national service is the only one which will give us that thrill of unity and vigor which we seek. An educational service built on the public school system puts the opportunity in our hands. The raw material in attitudes and desires is here. Every task that an army of youth might perform is already being done in some school or college or communal service. All we need to do is to coördinate and make universal what is now haphazard and isolated. An army of youth which focused school work would provide just that purpose that educators seek. The advocates of "preparedness" are willing to spend billions on a universal military service which is neither universal nor educational nor productive. Cannot we begin to organize a true national service which will let all serve creatively towards the toning up of American life?

X

THE SCHOOLS FROM THE OUTSIDE

To persons directing any complicated organization, criticism from outsiders always seems either futile or irrelevant. Conscious of the difficulty that has been met in creating the existing machinery, they resent the debonair and nonchalant proposals tossed in upon them by people who have only an amateurish or philosophical interest in their work. There are very few able administrators in any work who do not honestly believe they are doing their best with the material that is given them.

To this resentment the educational world seems particularly prone. The teacher finds it intolerable that the classroom should be judged from any vantage-point but the teacher's desk; the superintendent is annoyed if you arraign his system in the light of the product turned out. A public service which enlists so much conscientiousness as does our public school system is naturally sensitive to public criticism. Its very sensitiveness makes it difficult for it to distinguish between criticism of motives and criticism of policies and philosophies.

This resentment to amateur criticism is offset by an almost pathetic trust in expert overhauling. Letters from school principals to those in charge of recent investigations into city school systems imply that the expert has some kind of magical power not possessed by the ordinary teacher or administrator. When we learn, however, that the defects discovered are usually of so elementary and obvious a character that few interested laymen could have ignored them, we suspect that the magic is not so much a matter of the expert as it is of the outsider. The thing is to get a new point-of-view, a new interpretation, which shall not be so obsessed with the inside workings of the machinery that the drift of policy and the value of the human product is ignored.

Educators, it is true, "welcome fair criticism," and they have a fond belief that they get it from one another in the educational press. But in this mass of books and journals, crowded with exposition and discussion of current educational conceptions and technical methods, the whole setting, language, philosophy, are professional. The very bases and premises which the lay critic wishes to criticize are taken for granted. Educators decry "destructive" criticism, but in a sense all criticism is destructive, for it is essentially an examination. It requires a stripping away of the wrappings of routine and jargon, the turning of the idea about on all sides, the placing of it in a light where it may be clearly observed. There is another reason why amateur criticism is likely to be pertinent in education. The whole business of teaching and learning is a matter of personal psychology, and, in spite of current cant, there is no science so elusive and so unformulated as psychology. If the scientists will no longer deal with the problems of the personal, conscious life, it is left for the amateur philosophers to examine the psychological backgrounds of the teaching world, and attempt newer and more personal interpretations.

Much of the public criticism of the school is no doubt unintelligent, but what are we to say of that blanket defense we hear so often from the educator, that the niggardliness of the public prevents his providing the best schools and the best teachers? Now a country that attempts almost universally to provide free secondary school education—something provided in no European country—is certainly not thus guilty. The prestige of education in America is extraordinarily high. It is quite too late in the day to pretend that anyone still regards public schools as a charity, or that ridicule of teaching methods would only serve to discredit the schools and reduce the already small appropriations. There is no more fear—though some of our educators would have us believe it—that free criticism of the school will leave us school-less than there is that denunciation of the New York police resulted in leaving that city without police protection. The public schools in this country have the standing of all other public services.

It is not a question of more money, but of more intelligent use of present resources. The inexpert public cannot be expected to spend its money wisely. It has an incorrigible itch for objective results. It likes to see its money go into handsome buildings with expensive equipments. Large sums are spent in emulative waste. If one town boasts a seventy-five thousand dollar high school, its neighbor must have a hundred thousand dollar one. It is obvious that money which goes into costly ventilating systems and the adoption of uncriticized fads, does not go into teachers' salaries. But it is the function of the educators to offset this public childishness with their own wisdom, and see that the public money is profitably spent. If they believe that we could have better teachers if we paid more for them, they should see that the money goes to the teachers and not into fussy mechanical details.

The trend of educational activity has been to encourage this objective standard. More of the intellectual energy of the educational world has gone into technique and organization than into psychology. It has been more interested in seeing that the American child had enough cubic feet of air, a hygienic desk, and a fireproof building, than that he acquired an alert and curious outlook on the modern world, and an expressive personality. France, with public school buildings, even in Paris, that you would scarcely perhaps stable your horse in, somehow, by making expression the insistent motive of education, turns out intellectual products strikingly superior to our own.

European experience tends, too, to challenge the common assumption of American educators that quality of teaching is proportional to salaries paid. American salaries are certainly as high as those paid in European countries. There is no violent contrast, moreover, between the intellectual and educational background of a primary teacher with seven hundred a year and a principal with twenty-five hundred. They would both subscribe to the same philosophy of life; they might easily have come from the same training-school. The difference would be one of age or executive capacity, or of "experience," which generally means nothing more than greater expertness with routine and a longer setting of the intellectual cement.

It is this background, spirit, philosophy, behind the educational mind that the critical public is becoming more and more restless about. It does not challenge details of mechanical and administrative organization. These have been worked out with an ingenuity and a completeness all too thorough. The public is demanding now a similar attention to the conscious and spiritual side of learning and teaching. The ideal of the school as an embryonic community life, of the child as a growing personality to whom the activity of the school must have intense reality, of education as the training of expression, creation—this has hardly begun to be generally felt. The faults discovered by the Springfield and Portland school surveys arose largely from a careless and mechanical philosophy of life, an educational philosophy that had not sufficiently emphasized these ideals. The investigators were able, for instance, to tell on the moment whether a teacher had come from a certain training-school by her method and attitudes.

The responsibility cannot be dodged by the professional educators. They are responsible for primitive and mechanical attitudes which make so much of the orthodox public school teaching a mere marking of time rather than an education. Millions of the public's money would not effect this change in the background of the teaching world. That background could be changed without its costing the public a cent. The difficulty, huge, it is true, like any other attempt to change the obscure and uncriticized assumptions that lie at the bottom of any theory or practice, is psychological, not mechanical. It involves only the substitution, for certain undemocratic, ultra-logical ideas, of ideas more congenial to the time and social situation in which we live.

XI

THE PORTLAND SCHOOL SURVEY

If we are to have better schools in our cities we must know what kind of schools we have now. In an attempt to tell us, the school survey has in the last few years been developed with an admirable technique, and the passion for being surveyed has spread to cities large and small. No more illuminating document has come out of this effort than the recently published study of the school system of Portland, Oregon. It stirs enthusiasm because it shows the progress that has been made in clarifying the current problems and the ideals which must be realized if the public school is to prepare the child of to-day for intelligent participation in the society of which he will form a part. Compared with the investigations in New York City and Springfield, Illinois, this Portland survey, under the direction of Professor Cubberley of Stanford University, represents a new achievement in educational thinking. Those surveys contented themselves with a criticism of details, or, at best, with a vague groping for constructive plan. The Portland survey represents a definite break with the tradition. It is characterized by a clear idea not only of how the system fails to meet the modern demands, but of how these demands can be met.

The investigators cannot, of course, explain how it is that one of the wealthiest and most comfortable of American cities, a city at once entirely modern and homogeneously American, should have the most mechanical and formalistic school system these educators had ever seen. One gets the sense of how without leadership the school may become a little backwater in a community. In Portland, a city of 250,000 people, commercial and residential center for the great Northwest, these investigators found the "maintenance unchanged of a rigidly prescribed mechanical system poorly adapted to the needs either of children or community." "Universal practice," they say, "is enlisted in the maintenance of a rigid, minutely and mechanically prescribed system of instruction, organization, administration, supervision, examination and inspection. Any change in this elaborate mechanism meets with resistance, positive as well as negative. So far as this system is adapted at any point to the actual needs of the individual children and youth that come under it, so far as it is adapted to the needs of the communities for adequately trained recruits to serve the community, the adaptation is accidental, not the result of intelligence now operative at that point."

This is a criticism of an American institution, and Portland might be any large American city which has not had an educational awakening. The survey is significant because it shows the machinery and motives of public school education in this country for the last generation not only in Portland but in a city like New York, whose militaristic, mechanical system is now being thrown into convulsions by the sudden challenge of the new type of school embodied in the Gary plan. Indeed this Portland survey is a much better survey of New York school conditions than the elaborate Hanus inquiry which was made a few years ago.

The viciousnesses which the investigators found in the Portland system are those which are familiar to all who feel the defects of their own schooling, or have set about to examine the reasons for the poor quality of the school output. On the administrative side there are all the evils that come from retaining a scheme of amateur control in a system which has of necessity become professionalized. A board which is directing a village school must keep all school matters under its supervision. But when that village has become a vast city, a school board which keeps the strings in its own hands is simply manufacturing wastefulness and inefficiency. A lay board which employs highly paid and highly trained principals, supervisors, etc., and then insists on directing all business—from the engaging of janitors and the personal selection of teachers to the suspension of by-laws whereby a schoolroom may be leased for an evening lecture or a teacher excused to attend the funeral of her grandmother—labels itself as archaic and unfit. It is one of the cardinal principles of modern political and industrial organization that it is a waste of money to pay salaries large enough to buy judgment, discretion and expert skill and then not permit them to be used.

This refusal to delegate responsibility, the investigators found, paralyzed initiative all through the school system. Nothing could be done without reference to an untrained body of laymen who, however conscientious they might be, must usually decide spasmodically and without any definite educational policy. Indeed their conscientiousness is often a positive vice. Shiftlessness on their part would have permitted initiative on the parts of principals and teachers. Under present conditions the distinction between good teachers and bad fades out. The concern of every one becomes to keep the machinery going, not to criticize the work and keep it adapted to the individual aptitudes of the children.

This administrative lifelessness has its counterpart in a pedagogical routine the focus of which is the "course of study." The curriculum is uniform for all children. It is "vivisected into fifty-four dead pieces," laid down in pages in certain adopted textbooks. "The only thought devoted to the formulation of the course of study," say the investigators, "was the simple mathematical thought necessary to parcel out the pages of the books." The teacher's duty is to haul the pupil through the course of study. This is done by means of the formal recitation, where "pupils answer hollow word-questions with memorized hollow word-statements." Term examinations discover how many of these word-statements are left in the pupils' minds. An elaborate system of inspection and supervision exists to check up and grade both teachers and principals and ensure that the hallowed "course of study" is fully being carried out. Many of the teachers are trained in the local schools and turned back into the system to perpetuate these methods. A state tenure-of-office act keeps all teachers in their places.

The effect upon the children is logical. The school becomes an automatic process of elimination. Those who can be hauled through the course of study are hauled. Those whose talents do not lie in the capacity to memorize printed pages pass out of the school or become hopelessly mired in the lower grades. "If the sixteen-year-old child has not yet transferred to his memory Parts 37 to 54, inclusive, of the dead and comminuted curriculum, the chief constituents of which are abstract arithmetic and technical grammar, then he must begin with Part 37 and appropriate that and each of the succeeding 17 Parts in order, before he can even be associated with youth of approximately his own age, and before he can engage in study suited to his age and condition—study and exercises that will be of immediate and practical value to him in the effort he must shortly make to serve society for the sake of his own livelihood." And this system, formulated and approved twenty years ago by high educational authorities, the survey stigmatizes as valuable only in its "cheapness and facility of administration, and the relief that it affords educational officers and teachers from all responsibility of knowing and of meeting the individual needs of their pupils."

This type of public school, so bald and grotesque in the sober pages of the Portland survey that it seems more like the ritual of some primitive tribe than the deliberate educational activity of an enlightened American community, is yet the type that still prevails in the majority of our cities. This is the fact that we must face. Yet a community that asks to be surveyed is a community dissatisfied with itself. Other communities are likely to stir uneasily, and ask themselves why, if Los Angeles and Indianapolis and Gary can have modern and fruitful public school systems, other cities should not. We may even hope that it is the last of the old system and the promise of the school of to-morrow.

XII

WHAT IS EXPERIMENTAL EDUCATION?

At a time when more people are thinking intelligently about American education than ever before, it is unfortunate that there should be any confusion between the widely diverse trails that experimentation is opening up to the modern school. It is becoming increasingly evident that the "experimental" in education does not at all mean the same thing to educational administrators as it does to educational idealists. "Experimental education" has not yet been pitted in competition against the "experimental school," but it is not unlikely that the different techniques which they suggest may come to seem hostile to each other, and so the real values of both be lost. At present the two seem to be developing in a fairly complete disregard of each other. It would be dangerous for American education to tangle itself in the dilemma of choosing between them. On the other hand, it would be even more disastrous to confuse them. If we attempt to apply the quantitative standards of the new "experimental education" to the life of the "experimental school," or to infuse the qualitative ideals of the "experimental school" into the technique of "experimental education," we run the risk of spoiling that modern and socially-adjusted school towards which we are all feeling our way.

When the inventive school superintendent or professor of education speaks of "experimental education," he is thinking, not of the "model school," but of the new standard tests in the fundamental subjects by which the work of large masses of public school children is being regularly measured and compared. The city school survey has elaborated a technique of intellectual measurements which is giving us very rapidly a genuine quantitative science of education. A report like Professor Judd's in the "Cleveland Survey"—"Measuring the Work of the Public Schools"—is a storehouse of suggestiveness for all who like to see how mathematics can be fruitfully applied to living. These statistical studies measure accurately the performance of children in the different grades and at different ages in the specific literate skills which everybody needs even to start fairly in the race of opportunity. The standard tests have been worked out experimentally with great numbers of school-children so that average norms of accomplishment can be set for any class or any individual. Rates of speed and quality of handwriting, and their relation to each other; ability to spell common words; rate and capacity of accurate figuring; rate and quality of silent and oral reading;—these are the aptitudes that are rigidly measured by the tests. The children are treated as segregated arithmetical minds, reading minds, spelling minds, as units of intellectual behavior. The tests are not "examinations," for they do not aim to show any absolute attainment of "knowledge." Their value is in the comparison they afford of individual skill, and of deviations from a norm of effectiveness. In the mass of scores you have an intellectual relief map of your class, your school, your city system.

Now nothing could apparently be more deadly and mechanical than this treating of living children as if they were narrowly isolated minds. In this "experimental education" we are evidently in another world from the "experimental school." Yet out of these tests emerge the most important implications for modern education. Out of this "experimental education" we at last get a scientific basis for the "modern school." For we have irrefutable proof of the enormous diversity of minds and aptitudes. We have a demonstration of the utter foolishness of subjecting children to a uniform educational process. We have accurate proof of the fallacy of the "average" in education. These tests are added proof of the unscientific character of the typical public school on that very technical and administrative side which has been most carefully developed. The graded school was a brilliant invention for its time, but the bases of classification are shown by these new tests to be absurd. Children are now classified, for purposes of education, largely by age and average standing. The tests show that neither category has the slightest relevance for effective learning. We classify things for the purpose of doing something to them. Any classification which does not assist manipulation is worse than useless. But mere numerical age is no clue whatsoever to mental or even physiological age, and minds with the same average may plot out very differently for every individual one of the various skills and interests that elementary training involves. Our educational grading has been as sentimental and sterile as the ancient philosophers' classification of matter into earth, water, fire, air. Such a conception of the world was interesting, but there was nothing you could do with it. All the school has done with its classifying has been to get the children into groups where they could be dosed with an orderly sequence of lessons. There has been no handle by which their heterogeneous minds and wills could be taken hold of and directed. The rule of the classroom is necessarily military, because such diverse people could only be unified in the most objective and external and coercive way. No internal control would be possible. So the teacher must devote a large part of her educational energy to the mere business of policing. When she actually "taught," it was only the average child that she could really address—the fairly bright mediocrity. The other pupils wasted their time almost in direct proportion to their deviation above or below that average. Children passed up through their educational life on the basis of an "average mark," which represented nothing whatever but a number. The standard tests have shown repeatedly that ability is so unevenly distributed that the brightest fourth-year children overlap the poorest eighth-year children. However children may average, scarcely two children in the same class will ever be found to have the identical capacity in the different subjects. The tests reveal not only that children differ, but just how curiously and widely they do differ.

The traditional classification is enough to wreck any educational system, even without the deadness of the curriculum. With the progressive congestion of the public schools, teaching has become more and more impossible. The traditional system of grading has successfully resisted most improvement in teaching, and vitiated the newer values that have been brought into the school. If children, clearly not defective, cannot learn arithmetic, read slowly and unintelligently, spell chaotically and write a slovenly hand, question the grading system. Never have there been such admirable techniques for teaching these fundamental things. But the classification defies them. The "class" gives the teacher no leverage for improving the children's skill. An unscientific grading is as much a barrier to altering minds as it is to changing materials.

These truths seem elementary and obvious, yet we had to wait for this "experimental education" to shake complacency in the "graded school." Now if we accept these tests we have to conclude that it is useless to grade children for education unless those "grades" correspond accurately and specifically to the capacities of the children. Work must be done in each specific subject with—and only with—those who have approximately the same capacity. The "average" is totally unknown in that "real life" which we are constantly forced to set up in antithesis to the school. In no function of life is any one going to be judged by a composite ability to read, write, spell, figure. One succeeds not through any average skill or average information, but through the ability to throw all one's skill and all one's intelligence where it is demanded. A measurement of intelligence by averages will always produce just that ineffectiveness and vagueness for which the products of the public school are censured at present.

The fallacy of the educational "average" involves another fallacy, equally obvious but equally prevalent. This is the fallacy of the "partially perfect." The school ranks the seventy per cent. child equal to the hundred per cent. child. Children pass to more difficult work on an admitted basis of imperfect accomplishment. But for any real effectiveness in the world it is not enough to be habitually only seventy per cent. right. Whenever you need to be literate, the world demands that you be actually literate. If you have information, you are either useless or dangerous unless your information is accurate. It is better not to know arithmetic at all than persistently to make only seven hits out of ten. For all practical purposes your child is as much a failure at seventy per cent. as he is at zero per cent. It will avail him little to be able to read and write and figure at a rate and an excellence only seventy per cent. of the standard. In any situation which requires these elementary skills he will be almost as much handicapped as if he were entirely illiterate. It is time that the school faced the bitter truth that life demands an approximate perfection in whatever one tries to do. Education must shape all its technique towards this approximate perfection. It is not necessary that all should do the same thing. But it is necessary that what one pretends to do one should succeed gradually in doing. The individual who is allowed to persist continuously on a level of imperfect accomplishment is not being educated. For him education is a failure. He should either drop his technique, or ways should be found to improve him towards mastery. What children are learning at any one time they should be learning with a sense of control. The more difficult should not be confronted till the less difficult has been absorbed. And this controlled progress will be possible only in a school where children work with their equals. Classification in education should be based only on specific proficiency.

The new "experimental education" is engaged in making dramatic in the schools these truths. It is a force even more revolutionary than the idealism of the "experimental school." The situation suggested by the "curve of distribution" is one of the most momentous facts to be reckoned with by us of to-day. It is making over our theories of democracy, social reform and social progress. To work out its manifold implications in the school is to touch the very nerve of our democratic future.

XIII

THE ORGANIC SCHOOL

The Fairhope Summer School, which has just closed its season (Sept., 1915), at Greenwich, Connecticut, has given to Northern people an opportunity to see at work Mrs. Marietta Johnson's widely known ideal of "organic education." Just as the Gary plan has shown how the city school may give a varied training to great masses of children with a freedom and flexibility never believed possible, so Mrs. Johnson has demonstrated how the small community, or even household, by using the natural environment and the natural needs as laboratory and workshop, may adjust the child to life far more accurately than any formal school. No school carries out more carefully Professor Dewey's dictum that the child can only be educated by concerning himself with what has meaning to him as a child, and not what is to have meaning to him later as an adult.

In the organic school, children grow up naturally and healthfully, playing out-of-doors, following their curiosities, learning as their life makes demands upon them. The teacher is there to answer their questions, to sharpen their wits, to name for them and analyze the flowers and soil and trees, to show how to plant vegetables and build little coops or houses. In their winter school at the single-tax colony of Fairhope, Alabama, on the shores of Mobile Bay, the children can be out in the open air almost every day. The land is a complete geological, botanical, and physical laboratory, and the household a natural classroom where they learn to live. The school grew, in fact, quite naturally out of the household, and the necessity for some sort of school in a community where there was none. Mrs. Johnson, with her teacher's genius, simply sharpened and arranged her intercourse with the children around her, and presently had a school which has become one of the most interesting in the country.

Its very informality is its charm and success. The hundred or more children are not classified in grades, but in "life-classes," which correspond roughly to those three periods in child life—the first seven years of growth, the years to adolescence, and early adolescence. The first class is really an outgrowth of the nursery. In the cool rooms of the Fairhope Summer School one comes upon little farmhouses and villages and doll-houses of building-blocks, which form the basis for getting acquainted with the village the children lived in. The next group is characterized by a tough practicality, a capacity for drill and persistence, and this "life-class" was found in the wood-working shop and garden. Literary studies are taken up very late by the third class, whose recitations are rather informal discussions in an outdoor cluster around the teacher. Only when a broad background of acquaintance with real things is obtained, practical powers of observation acquired, and an actual need felt for learning what books can tell, are the conventional school studies begun. In the organic school there is thus some chance left to the children for getting real meanings and not mere words and phrases which they may glibly repeat. Reading and writing are not taught by drill, but are picked up by the child from the teacher or the other children, in the Rousseauan fashion, whenever he finds that he is missing something very important and interesting in not having this skill.

Learning in this kind of school becomes as natural as eating. One learns when one is hungry to understand what is going on in the world. Such schools, it will be said, are all very well as an ideal, but where can teachers be found to direct them? Certainly many of Mrs. Johnson's children could teach others in the way they have learned themselves. The way to get teachers for this free organic education in the "schools of to-morrow" is clearly to teach more children in the same way.

XIV

COMMUNITIES FOR CHILDREN

Mr. Wirt's schools at Gary are genuine public schools, in the sense that they provide for every kind of child in the community and draw into themselves the main aspects of the community life. They are not artificial training-schools for vocations or for life; they are a life itself. "The public school is still merely the old private school publicly supported," he says. The change of support has not really made it a different kind of a school. It has not really grown up to urban demands. School-boards usually act as if they were handling private property. They gravely discuss "wider use of the school plant" as if this were some gracious extension of privilege. The public does not yet feel that the schools are its own. Organization, administration, instruction, are highly authoritative, doctrinaire. The ideal has been uniformity in methods and product. The educational system has become as autocratic and military as the industrial. As for content, the curriculum is the old medieval one, not transformed, but patched up, in the good old Anglo-Saxon way, as interests which had been the concern of the few were gradually demanded by the many. Art study, nature study, physical education, science, organized play, manual training, have been added to the public school work. But these new interests and activities have become simply additional "subjects," taught in much the same spirit as the old. The problem of the educator has been, not how may the new activity vitalize and transform the others, but how can it be introduced with the least disturbance to what is already there. The present discussion of professional educators about vocational training shows the same mechanical effort to introduce an alien activity into the traditional curriculum in such manner that the latter may remain intact.

Mr. Wirt's own school is not a tinkering-up of the present school system. He is not an "educational reformer" making something over. He has plowed up the educational ground. He actually has a new kind of a school. It is not a "school of unspecialized vocational training," or "a school founded on play," or an "efficiency school," or any of the other terms with which it has been designated. It is hard to describe because it defies classification in the old terms. Nothing is more delightful about the Gary schools than the absence of cant. Most of the current educational problems, the books and ideas on pedagogy, educational psychology, supervision, administration, teaching-methods, classroom management, discipline, etc., which fill the attention of the current educational world are here as if they were not. It is a school built up outside the influence of the professors of education, the teachers' colleges, and the normal school of the land. It is true that there is probably not a single idea operative that is original with Mr. Wirt. Probably there is not a single idea that is not being applied in some school in the country. The novelty is the synthesis, and the democratic spirit that motivates it.

Here is provided for the first time a genuine public school, a school which does reflect all the healthy interests of the community, and where the child does become familiar with its life and with his own interests and vocational opportunities through practical doing of work. The school becomes "a clearing-house for community life." To enter the Emerson or Frœbel School in Gary—the two superb new buildings constructed by Mr. Wirt—is like coming into a well-ordered city where each citizen is going about his proper business. There is none of that slightly depressing atmosphere of the mild if excellent prison for half-day involuntary labor which is too often the ordinary school. Classes do not seem to be neatly immured in rooms, or to be moving about in lock-step. You are dealing with interested individuals who, singly or in spontaneous groups, are utilizing all the facilities of a lavishly equipped and stimulating community. The tone is of a glorified democratic club, where members avail themselves of privileges which they know are theirs. The schools are public in the same broad sense that the streets and parks are public. The school is the children's institution. They unaffectedly own it and use it as a mechanic uses his workshop or an artist his studio. To go to the schools in the evening and see the children running and playing in the great broad halls—incomparable playrooms—running in now and then to speak to their parents who are studying in the evening school, is to get a new emotional sense of what a school may be. The children do not seem to be there because education is "compulsory," or because the parents send them there to get rid of them, but because what can be done there is so interesting that they cannot stay away.

I am unable otherwise to account for their streaming back in such numbers to the voluntary Saturday schools, voluntary for the teachers, too, who are paid extra for their work. Saturday is a glorified pay-day, where one may do anything one likes, from making swords in the wood-shop to studying back work in the classroom. I spent a fascinating hour watching the thronged wood-shop where little boys were fussing with the scraps left from the regular work of the week. It occurred to me then how little real difference there was between the well-to-do home and the very poorest in the way of interesting activities for children. How many homes of the comfortably enlightened classes were fit places to bring up a child? How many even pretend to supply the books and the wood-work and tools and plants and music with which these wonderful buildings were running over? Without interesting activities for children, city homes, both rich and poor, can provide only schools for loafing. As between the street, to which the less well-to-do child emerges for interest, and the vaudeville, the "movie" and the current fads to which the well-to-do child escapes, I think the street is probably the less demoralizing.

This Saturday workshop was a little study in spontaneous discipline. Although the children were unwatched, they worked on their own little jobs as indefatigably as if they were under a drill-master. If any little boy became weary and was moved to interfere with another little boy, he was apt to be brushed off as though he were an irritating fly. Could it be that mischievousness, supposed to be an integral part of child-nature, was simply a product of repression or idleness? Could it be that school discipline was largely an attempt to solve problems which artificial rules were directly manufacturing? Visiting superintendents, appalled at the freedom in the Gary schools, tip-toe about looking for signs of depredation. They do not seem to report any. I decided that these schools had actually acquired the "public" sense. It seemed really true that children, unless they were challenged to inventive wickedness by teachers' rules and precepts, were no more likely to spoil their school than a lawyer is likely to deface the panels in the library of his club. This children's community seemed to be enjoying its busy life in the same spirit that the wider public uses its streets and libraries and museums and railroad trains.

This supremely democratic public sense is the motive of Mr. Wirt's genius. All this richness of opportunity—the playgrounds, gymnasia, swimming-pools, gardens, science laboratories, work-shops, libraries, conservatories—which this school provides so lavishly, is possible to the public of a small and relatively poor city like Gary, exactly because the schools are managed like any other public service. The modern educational ideal, "to provide a desk and seat for every child," is as absurd as would be one to provide a seat in the park for every inhabitant. No public service is used by more than a fraction of the people at any one time. Mr. Wirt provides the coveted "desk and seat" for about one-quarter of the children. While they are studying the traditional three R's, etc., the rest of the school is distributed in shop and playgrounds, gymnasium and studio, or at home. By an ingenious redistribution of the groups throughout the course of an eight-hour day, Mr. Wirt is able not only to give every child the opportunity of the varied facilities every day, but he is able to accommodate in one school building twice the ordinary number of children. The insoluble "part-time" problems of city schools disappear. The Gary school has two complete schools, each with its set of teachers, functioning together in the same building all day long. In the lower grades the child spends two hours daily in the classroom, an hour in laboratory or shop, half-an-hour in studio, and half-an-hour in gymnasium, an hour in auditorium, and the rest of the day in study, play or outside activity. The older child has three hours for formal instruction, and two hours for more intensive shop or studio work. Children are passing back and forth constantly between home and school, each with his or her own scheme of work, and all the school is being used all the time.

The amount of money thus saved in school buildings alone is so large that even a town like Gary, with relatively meager school revenues, can afford not only the varied equipment, but also luxuries like special school physicians and nurses, and special teachers for special subjects. Mr. Wirt has been accused of "business efficiency," but this is scarcely the term for so artistically elegant a scheme of economy. When you reflect that it is just because the traditional classrooms are provided for only a proportion of the children that all of them have the varied daily opportunities of many-sided work and play, you are likely to call this "economy," in the old golden Greek sense of the wise management of household resources, so that every member may share alike in the activity and the wealth. Such economy is creative; it enriches, not impoverishes. I have said that Mr. Wirt thought in terms of the rural community, but it is of the rural community and its creative economy, expanded to fill and reorganize the life of the modern city. The school trains the child by letting him do the things the city does. His education is an acclimatization to the wider social life.

A truly public school would let nothing communal remain alien to itself. In the chemistry class at the Emerson School I actually found the children helping in the necessary chemical work for the city. The class was simply an extension of the municipal laboratory. Gary, of course, has the good fortune or the good sense to have as chemistry teacher the municipal chemist. The older children act as his assistants. With him the class tests the city water, the various milk supplies of the town. Under the inspector, they visit dairies, workshops, bakeries and food-stores. Last year they published a milk bulletin containing general information and reports of their tests. I could not see that it was essentially inferior in quality to one that an agricultural school might have issued. When I came upon this class it was testing sugars and candies, from the different shops of the town, for purity and for use of coloring matter. Another class was experimenting with soft drinks, studying questions of solution, suspension and crystallization, with ramifications, I was told, towards the physiological effect of certain products. The children were practically deputy food inspectors, and made reports on the official blanks. The chemist assured me that he had not lost a case in prosecuting for violation of the pure food laws. In East Chicago, where school-children were ostensibly not trained as a vigilance committee in scientific investigations, the chemist could not get a single conviction.

The children also test the materials supplied to the school, the coal, cement, etc., to see whether they come up to specifications. I saw a group trying to make soap for the use of the school. The chemist assured me—college-trained ignoramus that I was amidst this youthful expertness—that there was scarcely a principle of the science, theoretical or practical, that he could not develop from this work, all so directly motivated by the daily life around the children. I wish I could convey the fine caliber of this young chemist as he stood in his laboratory with the children working around him, his clear poise between the theoretical and the practical making him for me the ideal symbol of science working ceaselessly at the world around to make it cleaner and healthier and more livable.

That chemistry class in Gary has a high and momentous significance to me. It was distinctly not play, as all other laboratory work in school or college that I have seen has been play. I was surprised to find how completely the doing of real work banished the amateur atmosphere and at the same time made the work infinitely more interesting. Mr. Wirt says the child is a natural scientist, indefatigably curious and resourceful, quick and accurate. The little children actually seem to achieve less breakage than the older. What kind of a community we are going to have when any large proportion of the children grow up to observe and test the physical conditions under which they live—when they get the scientific-deputy-inspector habit, so to say—and what would happen to some forms of political jugglery if a younger generation got used to thinking in terms of qualitative and quantitative tests, I leave to the imagination. But it seemed to me that that chemistry class was one of the most important activities in the United States to-day.

XV

REALLY PUBLIC SCHOOLS

Characteristic of the "public sense" of the Gary schools is the class in history and geography, which I found at work getting an imaginative background of the larger social world. To the news-board in the hall they brought clippings that seemed important. The history room was smothered in maps and charts, most of them made by the children themselves. There was a great red Indiana ballot, a chart of the State Senate, a diagram of State administration, a table showing the evolution of American political parties, war-maps and pictures. The place was a workshop, with broad tables for map drawings, and a fine spread of magazines and papers. "Laboratory" work in history, tried so timorously in some of our most daring colleges, was in full swing in a Gary high school class.

When I visited the room the class was concerning itself with reports on "The city as a healthful place to live in," with special emphasis on parks, because the town had been waging its campaign for the new water-front park. Little outlines on Greek and Roman cities, medieval and modern cities, had been worked up in the school library—bountifully equipped as a branch of the city public library. I had walked into a true course on town-planning, at once the most fascinating and significant of current social interests and the study that packs into itself more historical, sociological and geographical stimulation than almost any I know. A class that had gone through those reports would have the materials for exactly the social background that our current imaginations need; and, moreover, all those materials would be firmly placed in the community setting.

There is a charming communal self-consciousness about Gary, and this sort of history is the thing that feeds it. One class had been working on a comparison of Athenian and Spartan education with Gary education. This struck me as peculiarly delightful. Such social introspection we rather badly lack in America, yet it is the only soil in which intellectual virtue can ever grow. The ancient history class has for its purpose: "to improve its members as American citizens by a study of the experiences of the ancient peoples." This class, after some classroom turbulence, formed a voluntary society which is duly opened and conducted by the president, while the instructor lingers in a leisurely fashion outside. I know of no more admirable reason for historical study than this phrase, the natural expression of the Gary child who wrote the constitution for this class.

They do not seem to know whether they are studying "Civics" or not. They are too busy soaking in from real events a familiarity with history as it is lived and the community as it works. I throw in here an advertisement for the "Literary Digest" and the "Independent," which the pupils regularly read. They study history backward, so that it explains what is happening to-day. They repeatedly dramatize remote times. They are talking of coöperating with the State historical pageant. It seemed to me that these children were actually learning their social world in the spontaneous natural way that the intelligent child learns it from newspapers and books and from the slow, unconscious widening of horizon for which he must usually look quite outside the school.

If other community institutions have anything educational to offer outside the school, or if parents and children think they have, Mr. Wirt's school lets the children go to these out of their auditorium or play hour. The churches may have them for religious instruction—there is no Bible-reading or prayer in the Gary schools—and thus avoid the imagined necessity for a special kind of church day-school. Already a Polish parochial school in Gary has lost its reason for being and vanished. Y. M. C. A.'s, neighborhood houses, special music-teachers, etc., may also act as extensions of the school. It will be interesting to see how successfully some of these institutions which purport to form the child's morals and care for his soul's destiny prove their supplementary value, and how far they are not simply having joyfully extended to them a long rope by which they may hang themselves.

To Mr. Wirt the school is not more a community than the community is a school. He believes that parks and playgrounds should follow the schools, and in Gary he demands twenty acres for every school plant. He does not rely upon public playgrounds, to which, as experience shows, only a proportion of children can be enticed from the streets, but his playground is a part of the school on equal terms with the other activities. Otherwise these very expensive grounds which cities are providing are apt to be futile. Mr. Wirt's policy is to make it as easy as possible for the community to use the schools. He does not force people to the opportunities, but he puts them where the people cannot easily evade them. He does not drive children to the public library, but he has a branch put in each school. The Gary schools are open night and day, practically every day in the year. The Indiana law—protector from tyranny—forbids more than ten months of school a year, but allows vacation schools. Sunday sees popular lectures. The Gary schools seem almost as public as the streets.

If the school is to be not only a community embryonic of current society but also a school-community of itself, it must have some forum or theater where everything that is peculiarly interesting in any part of the school may be brought dramatically to the attention of the rest of the school. This Mr. Wirt provides in the auditorium hour, so drearily used in the ordinary school for religious exercises, "speaking pieces," and moral homilies. In Gary every child goes to "auditorium" for an hour each day, but he listens there to talks by the special teachers about their work, lantern-lectures and dramatic dialogues written by the children themselves from their history or literature work. There may be moving-pictures, instrumental music, gymnastic exhibitions. The initiative and responsibility are left to the teachers. There seems to be no limit to the interest and the possibility of what may go on in this free little secular theater except what the imagination of teachers and children can suggest. There is always singing, and of a most excellent tone. "Auditorium" is one of Mr. Wirt's novel ideas. It seems to make unreal the old categories of "entertainment" and "edification," just as the rest of the school seems to damage the conceptions of "work" and "play." There was a pleasant informality about things, with the girls sewing at the back of the theater, and the young audience breaking into whistling as they marched out to the music of the piano. "Auditorium" ought to be quite as important as Mr. Wirt thinks it is. What school-work might become, lived always in the possible light of its intelligent presentation to the school audience in dramatic form, we do not know, because educators have never been dramatists. The Gary schools have special teachers for expression, but the American spirit is in many ways so inexpressive that the idea can thus far be only a frank and delightful experiment.

I liked particularly in the "auditoriums" I visited the intermingling of children of all ages. This is one of the many ways by which the Gary school breaks down the snobbery of age which causes so much unhappiness in childhood, and fixes the adult mind with so many delusions. I came across a significant editorial in the Emerson School paper which showed me how useful this intermingling was in smashing caste lines that were already forming. The editor acknowledged that the expected objectionableness of the "youngsters" had not asserted itself. One got a real sense of a new sympathy breaking upon these already sophisticating minds of high-school children.

I mention this because it is typical of Mr. Wirt's genius to obliterate artificial lines and avoid mechanical groupings. His ideal school is one like the Emerson in Gary, a complete school, from kindergarten to college, in the same building, with all the varied facilities used by all classes. The grading is of the utmost flexibility. The traditional twelve grades are followed, but classes work in "rapid," "average," or "slow" groups, according as the various children give promise of completing the State-prescribed curriculum in ten, twelve or fourteen years. The child may pass from group to group or from grade to grade at any time on the examination of the supervisor of instruction. The child himself has no sense of being "graded" or even "marked." Report-cards are rather a concession to parents' weaknesses. If the child needs additional help, there is the parallel school, so that he may have a double lesson the same day. And the Saturday school offers another opportunity.

All studying is supposed to be done in school hours. The fearful bogey of "home-work" is laid. In this free interchange of groups the child acquires a sense of individuality. Each has practically an individual schedule of work, for the organization of which the executive principal, who devotes all his time to such matters, is responsible. Except in the youngest classes, the children seem to move about individually to their different rooms and shops. By this drastic carrying down of college methods through the grades Mr. Wirt has exploded another hoary superstition that great masses of children in city schools can only be handled by uniform and machine methods, in a lump. Frœbel School in Gary has twenty-five hundred children, most of them very small alien immigrants. Yet the same flexible and free methods are used there, apparently with success. These children, because of the immensely varied equipment, and the possibility of small classes in the shops, are getting something resembling individual instruction. I picked up at random the card of an older girl at Emerson. It read: "Printing, History, Gymnasium, French, Music, Botany, Auditorium, English." The very shock of that bold "Printing" gives you a realization of the modern school you are in. And this is a girl besides.

Now a program like this, and all this free election and flexibility, would seem wilful and anarchical were it not for the fact that in the Gary school these schedules are the result of a natural and very careful process of selection, made by the child. What the child shall study, outside of the regular classroom work, is neither forced upon it nor aimlessly selected. Take the Emerson School, a beautiful building with laboratories and studios, gymnasia and shops, and put your child into its kindergarten or first grade. He runs about the halls. The shops and studies and laboratories are not segregated, but distributed over the building so as to convey the impression that they are equally significant, and to give every child an opportunity of becoming familiar with them. All the rooms have big glass doors or windows. The child's own unaided curiosity makes him look in and wonder about what the older children are doing there. One could see children of all ages peering into the foundry or machine-shop or printery.

When the child has reached the third or fourth grade he has a certain idea of what activity interests him, and he is allowed to go into shop or laboratory as observer or helper to the older child. He watches and asks questions, and the older boy learns by teaching him. If the child finds that the work does not actually interest him he still has the chance to change. When he takes up the work in the higher grades he has served his apprenticeship and is already familiar with the apparatus and the technique. The teacher does not have to break in a new class each year. It is almost a self-perpetuating and self-instructing class. The child has been assimilated to the work as new members in any profession or trade in society are assimilated. When the child is exposed from his earliest years to the various vocational activities, is allowed to come into them just as his curiosity ripens, you have as perfect a "choice of a vocation" as could be imagined. Only this sort of opportunity can really be called "vocational training." The usual vocation school work takes the child too late, when his curiosity is likely to be dulled; it puts him into the work without any previous familiarity. It can scarcely be anything but drudgery. If "capacities are to be developed," Mr. Wirt's scheme gives the surest means of developing them. It solves the grave problems of "vocational" and "pre-vocational" training, which are so sorely vexing the professional educational world, a large part of whose business in life seems to be to create and have problems.

XVI

APPRENTICES TO THE SCHOOL

Vocational training in the schools of Gary means that whatever work is necessary in the way of repairing, conserving, beautifying or enhancing the facilities, is done by the school itself. These large, lavishly equipped modern school-buildings require a force of mechanics to keep them in repair. Their shops are the industrial and manual shops for the school. The children work in them with skilled union workmen, who are employed not primarily as "manual training" teachers, but as assistants to the building superintendent. The mechanics teach by allowing the children to help them as apprentices. They earn their salaries by repair and construction work, while the children who desire it get an incomparable vocational training at practically no cost to the town. Where the ordinary trade-school must have large classes to make the enterprise pay, the Gary vocational work may be done with the smallest groups, for the shops are paying for themselves anyway.

Manual training takes on quite a new meaning as you move about, watching the boys in the carpenter-shop making desks or tables, or cabinets for the botany collections, or book-racks for the library, sending them on to the paint-shop when they have finished; boys in the sheet-metal shop hammering zinc for the roof; young electricians repairing bells; a couple of plumbers tinkering with pipes; little groups of serious and absorbedly interested boys in foundry and forge and pattern-making shop, all coöperating like the parts of a well-ordered factory. There was obviously enough real work to keep busy for his hour a day every child who desired training in a trade. Where school and workshop are thus fused, the need for "continuation" and "coöperative" courses—where the boy alternates between shop or factory and school—disappears. The child has the advantages of both.

The ordinary school, and even the specialized vocational school, is rarely doing more in its industrial, manual, or domestic science work than playing a rather dreary game with toys. There could scarcely be a greater contrast between the real shops of the Gary schools and those ordinary "shops" and kitchens with their dozens of little machines at which at a given time the entire class does its little stereotyped "stunt." In Gary the domestic science room is a real kitchen in which the daily luncheon is prepared and served at cost to the teachers and pupils who desire it. The cook is a real cook, and the girls come in as observers, helpers or workers, just as the boys go into the shops. The nearest approach to a luxury is the pottery shop, but this is itself perhaps the best symbol of that fusion of the artistic and the practical that is the Wirt genius. What are you to say when you walk into the art studio and find a dozen girls and boys high on a scaffolding painting a frieze which they have themselves designed, while others are at work on stained-glass designs to go in varnished paper on the panels of the door?

There is a genial, joyous quality about all the work that gives every room a charm—the foundry with its deep shadows, the smooth gray pottery shop with its turning wheels and bright glazed jugs, the botany room with its mass of greenery. Even the history room at Emerson School had the atmosphere which comes from concentrated interest and the slow accretion of significant material. Emerson itself is a spacious and dignified building with innumerable little touches of taste that one usually associates only with the high schools of exceptionally wealthy and cultivated suburban communities. It is a delightful paradox that so beautiful a life should appear to be lived where every activity seems to be motivated by direct utilitarian application. I said that you have to plow your mind up to understand this kind of a school. Certainly I have never seen a place which more nearly permitted to seem real that old ideal of the joy of work which we imagine must have existed back in guild days. It may be left to the imagination what children trained in such a school are likely to have to say to the industrial society in which we live.

The practical work of the school is only limited by local school needs, but the shoeless condition of some of the Frœbel children inspired the starting of a shoe shop where old shoes were made over. Both Emerson and Frœbel have a printery from which come all the blanks, reports, programs, etc., used in the school, as well as the bulletins and papers by which the various classes are tempted to preserve the good things they write. The commercial pupils have charge of all the accounting and bookkeeping as well as the supplies. The children who work in the shops are paid in checks, which are calculated on the basis of prevailing union wages for the working-time. This provides opportunities for a banking system, which is also in charge of the commercial class. In the Jefferson School the boiler-room is an integral part of the machine-shop.

The botany class was responsible for the beautiful and elaborate conservatory at the entrance of the Emerson School, and for the window hothouse in the botany room, where practical experiments are made. The botanists also have charge of the shrubs and trees on the grounds, and the vegetable gardens which they work communistically all through the summer. Their study of food and textile products ramified into the domestic science work, just as the zoology study was fused with physiology. This latter class had a playground zoo, with foxes and coyotes, raccoons and prairie-dogs, about whose habits and adventures they were preparing a brochure, which was already in press at the printery. When I stepped into the zoology laboratory itself, I found that I was in an even more animated zoo. Crows, chickens and pigeons in cages at the back of the room were lusty with vociferous greeting. The imperturbability of the children amidst this racket showed me how well aware they were that this was the way a zoology room ought to behave.

Such a school, where the child works almost unconsciously into a vocation which appeals to him as neither play nor drudgery, is far more "vocational" than even the specialized school. The child, beginning so young in shop or laboratory, and assimilating the work very gradually, is able to lay deep foundations of interest and skill. The Gary school is distinctly unspecialized. In a sense it gives a completely "liberal education." The child emerges a skilful amateur. The industrial and scientific work no more "train" him to take a definite place in the industrial world than the cultural work trains him to be a college professor. But he should leave school well equipped to cope with a dynamic, rapidly changing industrial society which demands above all things versatility, and which scraps methods and machines as ruthlessly as it does men. Only the man of rounded training and resourcefulness who can turn his hand quickly to a variety of occupations has much chance of success. Our public school, in spite of its fancied "liberal" curriculum, has really been turning out only very low-grade specialists. It has made no effort to produce the type of mind most needed to-day—the versatile machinist, the practical engineer, the mind that adapts and masters mechanism. This is probably the best intellectual type our society produces. This exactness, resourcefulness, inventiveness, pragmatic judgment of a mechanism by its product, the sense of machinery as a means, not an end, are exactly the qualities that society demands in every profession or trade.

The Gary school is the first I have seen that promises to cultivate this kind of intelligence. It frankly accepts the machine not in the usual sense of the vocational schools, as an exacting master that the child is to learn docilely to obey, but as the basis of our modern life, by whose means we must make whatever progress we may will. The machine seems to be a thing to which society is irrevocably pledged. It is time the school recognized it. In Gary it is with the child from his earliest years. It is the motive of his scientific study. The physics teacher at the Emerson School told me that he thought the fascinating and irresponsible automobile had done more to educate the younger generation than most of the public schools. Tinkering with an automobile was a whole scientific training.

I dropped into his physics class, and found a dozen twelve-year-old girls and their nine-year-old "helpers" studying the motor-cycle. With that fine disregard for boundaries which characterizes Gary education, the hour began with a spelling lesson of the names of the parts and processes of the machine. After the words were learned, the mechanism was explained to them as they pored over it, and their memory of vaporization, evaporation, etc., called into play. The motor-cycle was set going, the girls described its action, and the lesson was over, as perfect a piece of teaching as I have ever heard. The intense animation of that little group was all the more piquant for having as a background the astounded disapprobation of three grave school superintendents from the East.

To these physics classes the ventilating, heating and electric systems in the schools are all text-books. The climate is studied. The shops provide many physics problems. There was a class of boys having explained to them the physical principles of various types of machines. The impetuous rush of those little boys as they were sent into the machine-shop to take apart a lawn-mower, a bicycle, and a cream-separator, and the look of elation on their faces, would alone make Gary unforgettable to me. It was evident that this was indeed a different kind of school.

XVII

THE NATURAL SCHOOL

A surprisingly small amount of administrative machinery for so varied a system is required by the schools of Gary. Mr. Wirt is the City Superintendent of Schools. Under him each of the five school buildings has an executive principal. Two supervisors of instruction look after the pedagogical work of the system. The director of industrial work has charge of building repair, and supervises the shops where the children work under the mechanic-teachers. There is no attempt to segregate the vocational work. Manual, physical, artistic and academic activities are administered on an equal footing.

For the teacher the Gary school should be almost as liberating as it is to the pupil. In the details of courses much initiative is left to the teacher. It is really an inductive school where courses are worked out by supervisors consulting together on the basis of classroom experience. Teachers are encouraged to experiment and develop their own ideas. Here is the first public school I have ever seen that resolutely sets itself against uniformity of method or product, that recognizes differences of individuality.

The working-day of the teacher may be longer, but she is relieved of the burdensome home-work. The nervous strain is lessened also by the freer method of discipline. There cannot be unruly children unless children are ruled, and in the Gary school there is apparently no artificial repression. One found in the classroom as much talking as there would be in a concert audience, with the same natural motives, freed of "rules of order," for quiet. The frequent change of room and activity in the Gary school prevents, too, that nervous restiveness which must inevitably come to the child kept long at his desk. The point is that only in a free and varied school like this can one talk of effective discipline. When school activities are as attractive as they are here, deprivation becomes punishment. There is at hand an instrument for inculcating reason into refractoriness which is as powerful as the stoutest disciplinarian could wish. The ordinary school tries to keep up a military system of control, without any means, now that corporal punishment is generally abolished, of punishing infractions. In a Gary school "being sent home" for misbehavior usually means being sent to a place infinitely less interesting. But there is little talk about "mischievous and unruly boys." Those children who, in spite of everything, "are not adapted to our kind of school," may go to the school farm in the country to work. But this farm is not in any sense a "reform" school. Delicate children may also be sent there, and other classes go for a holiday. As to the personal manners prevailing in such a free school as this, with its absence of moral homily, and effort to "train character" through obedience and discipline, I can only repeat the words of an Italian boy who had recently come from orthodox schools elsewhere: "But they're so polite!"

I was glad to see that there was no nonsense at Gary about schemes of "self-government," which can be little more than a humiliating pretension in any school. A kindly judge did once institute "Boyville" in a Gary school, with a parody of municipal functions, but its unreality soon relegated it to limbo. Spontaneous organization there is, but it grows out of real work. The boys' ninth grade English class, for instance, has organized itself as the Emerson Improvement Association, and its work revolves around the speaking and writing necessary in conducting the affairs of the organization. There seem to be no "extra-curricular" activities, which create so many problems elsewhere. Athletic teams and sports are connected with the gymnasium work. Other societies spring up naturally out of the school interests. Problems of "fraternities" and the control of athletics which confront so many high schools are thus naturally avoided.

The Gary school not only lightens this strain of discipline for the teacher and cultivates her initiative, but serves as a kind of training-school for the teachers themselves. The new-coming teacher learns by acting as helper or "apprentice" to the older teacher, just as the children in shop or laboratory learn from one another. The result is an uncommon and appealing equality between teachers and children, without imposed authority on one side or subservience on the other. Beside Mr. Wirt Mme. Montessori seems almost a beginner, so daringly has he carried the principles of self-instruction up through the higher grades. Even visiting teachers and superintendents who wish to learn the theory and practice of the Gary school must learn in the same way. Mr. Wirt does not lecture to them. He allows them also to come into the school for a few months as helpers to teacher or principal. Everybody who has anything to do with a Gary school must evidently learn by doing the real work itself. Nothing shows more clearly the whole-knit fiber of Mr. Wirt's philosophy than this new kind of "normal" school for visiting teachers.

I was pleased with the absence of self-display. Advertising has come from the outside. The teachers seem innocent of the great number of things they are doing which a large part of the orthodox educational world believes to be impossible. You are talked with frankly and genially, but nothing is done to impress you. You are left to interpret it all for yourself. Those who miss the spirit will find weaknesses. Professional educators hold up hands of horror at the "looseness" of the teaching. They miss the dramatic effect of the "well-conducted recitation"—the drawing-out of the pupil's memory, or the appeals to glib guesses at what the teacher wants. They judge by the old-fashioned standard of how the teacher is teaching rather than the new one of what the child is learning. My complaint would be rather that there was still too much teaching that is conventional, particularly in the lower grades. And I have an animus against the deadly desks and seats which are still in use in too many of the classrooms. But the significant thing is that this kind of a school is not static or completed, but a constantly growing organism. The only limit to which it may grow lies in the imagination and initiative of teachers and pupils. And the school cannot be judged in cross-section. Even when it starts with so admirable an equipment, its life has just begun. For the mechanical and artistic, manual work and intellectual study, are all directed towards enriching the physical body and the spiritual life and atmosphere of the school. This intensive cultivation of resources produces that "embryonic community life" which is Professor Dewey's ideal, where in actual work the child senses the occupations and interests of the larger society into which he is to enter.

Mr. Wirt's schools would be unworthy of discussion were they not capable of imitation generally in American towns and cities. Already a number of communities have copied the essential features, and Mr. Wirt is at present occupied in remodeling a few of the New York City schools, successfully, too, in spite of the fact that New York, on account of its rapid growth, its great alien population, and its political cross-currents, presents perhaps the most formidable school problems in the country. The only substantial difficulty in remodeling schools according to the Gary scheme is the matter of playgrounds. Even this is surmountable, for most cities have parks or usable vacant lots within reach of the school. Mr. Wirt's great triumph in Gary is the old Jefferson School which he found when he came to the town. This was an orthodox ten-room building built by the city fathers to accommodate Gary children for many generations. By turning the spacious attic into a gymnasium, transforming five of the classrooms into music and art studios and nature-study laboratories, by building a jack-of-all-trades workshop around the engine-room in the cellar, a domestic-science kitchen in an unused corner, and by appropriating a nearby park space, he transformed a perfectly ordinary school building, whose prototype may be found in every town in the land, into a full-fledged, varied and smoothly-functioning Wirt school. Through the "rotation of crops" system, this school, built for three hundred and sixty children, actually accommodates over eight hundred, and gives them every facility, if less elaborately, of the specially designed new schools.

Perhaps I may here recapitulate. The mere prosaic business economy of the Wirt scheme is enough to recommend it. No school board can afford to neglect a plan which not only saves money to the taxpayers, but provides better facilities, more varied equipment and better educational opportunities than even well-to-do communities can at present afford. The Wirt school solves the vexing "part-time" problem. Gary is the only city I know that has room (March, 1915) in its present buildings for at least one-third more children than there now are to go to school.

In the second place, the plan solves most of the problems of vocational and industrial training which now confront the public school. It catches the child's curiosity and skill on the upstroke. It makes no separation of manual from intellectual work, and avoids that sinister caste-feeling which seems to be creeping into the vocational movement. And from the point of view of economy again, the scheme of devoting industrial work to actual care of the school-plant enables the school to provide a great variety of occupations almost without additional cost to the community.

In the third place, the plan provides a large measure of individual instruction. It is a school for every kind of a child. The flexibility of schedules, the coöperation of outside agencies like the churches, the varied activities, give opportunity for the fullest development of differing interests and capacities.

In the fourth place, the plan carries out throughout the school life the educational truth that learning can only come through doing. The habits and attitudes of careful scientific observation, or purposeful interesting activity which is neither work nor play, the social, democratic, and coöperative background which such a school cultivates, are exactly the qualities we need for our younger generation in American society.

Such a school carries out the best ideals of American democracy, as I see them, in an extremely effective way. Its philosophy is American, its democratic organization is American. It is one of the institutions that our American culture should be proudest of. Perhaps professional educators, accustomed to other concepts and military methods and administrative illusions, will not welcome this kind of school. But teachers hampered by drill and routine will want it, and so will parents and children.

XVIII

THE DEMOCRATIC SCHOOL

A recent article in the "New York Times" (Oct. 17, 1915) by Dr. Thomas S. Baker, Headmaster of the Tome School, contains an able pedagogical criticism of the Gary school which is typical of the general attitude towards the Gary idea on the part of conservative schoolmen. Nothing could bring out more clearly the difference in educational values between this professional teaching opinion and the broad social vision of Superintendent Wirt. Dr. Baker admits the impressive social effectiveness of the plan. It is "the last development in socializing the schools." Mr. Wirt is "not only an educator, but also a social reformer, a city worker." But Dr. Baker's argument is really the specialized pedagogical one against the social. Where Mr. Wirt sees the school as a community center, a children's world, Dr. Baker sees it as an educational factory. "The social value of the Gary schools," he says, "is beyond question. Its pedagogic excellence has still to be determined." From his point of view, a school is not so much a place to train effective citizens as to make "thorough scholars." He questions whether "these side issues in the scheme of child-training"—the gymnasia, shops, laboratories, which the Gary school contains—"are really essential in mental development." He is afraid that the young citizens of Gary learn more from their industrial shops and science laboratories than from their books.

Dr. Baker's guarded argument is really a glorification of "intellectual discipline" as against an intelligent capacity to lead an organic life in a modern society which needs above all things resourceful adaptation and social appreciations. It is a question of ideals, and no more important issue was ever put to a people than this one of how we want our next generation trained. The school is not only the one institution which assimilates all the people, but it is the most easily modifiable. It is not only the easiest lever of social progress but the most effective, for it deals with relatively plastic human material. To decide what kind of a school we want is almost to decide what kind of a society we want.

If we only want that kind of a school which would "make hard-working and accurate scholars and produce thoughtful men," we must resign ourselves to a progressive softening of the fiber and capacity of the mass of our people. The average educator acts as if he thought of his child-world as a level plain of capacities. There is the mass of unskilled, unawakened minds; here is the level of scholarship, knowledge, civic virtue, appreciations. Education is to him the process of lifting up the mass from their primitive level to the higher one. The public school is the elevator into which all are to be shoveled and transported to the upper story. And the American public school in the last fifty years has been faithfully following this ideal.

The truth is, of course, that mental aptitude is not any such level desert, but rather a series of inclined planes. When we try to educate all the children of all the people, we are not dealing with a homogeneous mass, but with sliding scales of capacity. A mental test of the school-children of a state would reveal an incline extending in orderly gradation from the genius down to the imbecile. A physical test would give us a different slant, a test for artistic or mechanical capacity another. Stand at the center of divine average and try to lever any of these slopes into a horizontal position and you find half of your society squatting heavily at the lower end. You may ascribe it to race capacity, personal heredity, social environment, malnutrition, defective nervous organization or anything you please, but the fact remains that the greater part of the human raw material will be permanently resistive to or only dully appreciative of any attempts to elevate them to a level. This is true of any capacity you may choose. The outstanding truth of society seems to be the heterogeneous distribution of capacities. And the irony of it is that after artistic capacity true intellectual capacity is probably the rarest. For the public school to try to make intellectualists of all its children is a sheer defiance of sociological reality.

Some educators, while they recognize this diversity, yet insist on uniform standards, uniform curricula, uniform discipline, on the ground that social order in a democracy is imperiled unless the highest degree of like-mindedness prevails. Such a democracy would be the stagnant democracy of China. The result of these attempts at standardization have been the automatic centrifugal flinging off into space of the children whose interests were not intellectual, who were no more capable of being made into "accurate scholars" than they were into artists and poets. And from those who did not get quite flung off, but clung on with their teeth, we get most of our prevailing pseudo-culture. To keep on trying to "develop the mind" and produce "thorough scholarship" in those whom we force to submit to educational processes, means simply to go on creating a nerveless and semi-helpless mass of boys and girls who will never take their effective and interested place in the world because they have no mental tools which they can wield. Such a course is coming to be generally recognized as a kind of slow national suicide, a slow suffocation of industrial and social progress.

The schools do change, but the schoolmen yield grudgingly. Nothing could be more naïve than the test which Dr. Baker proposes for evaluating the Gary plan. Submit, he says, the highest class in the Gary schools to an examination by the College Examining Board. If the students pass, the Gary system will be justified of its children. Was ever a more patent assertion of the professional bias? Let the children drop out of the lower grades untrained except in the rudiments, but if the small minority in the highest class passes its Vergil and algebra and English literature and German with marks as high as the graduates of the Tome School, then the Gary system will cease to be considered a "mere experiment." If this is what the critics of the Gary plan mean when they plead for an "evaluation of this novel experiment," we may well hope that it will escape the peril.

Such a conception of educational values cannot become too speedily obsolete. A public school is a mockery unless it educates the public. It cannot make the rarefied and strained product at the top the test of its effectiveness. And the public is not ideally educated unless its individuals—all of them—are intelligent, informed, skilled, resourceful, up to the limit of their respective capacities. Life itself can no longer be trusted to provide this education; the school must substitute. The Gary school deliberately sets such an ideal. Democracy does not mean uniformity, but it does mean equality of opportunity. A democratic school would be one where every child had the chance to discover and develop aptitude. The Gary school, with its harmonious activities of intellectual, manual, artistic and scientific work, physical education and play, gives just this chance. Democratic education does not mean the provision of separate schools for different kinds of children, or even separate courses in the same school, as the movement for industrial education is now threatening to bring. This is to create at once invidious distinctions, and fasten class education upon us. To say that children are different does not mean that some are fitted to be scholars and others to be manual workers, some to be artists and some to be scientists. The differences are differences of focus and not of quality.

To most children will appear in the course of school life some dominant interest, and it is upon the cultivation of that interest that the child's chance of being more than a nerveless mediocrity will depend. It is upon that training that his chance of being absorbed out of the school into the social and industrial world will depend. At the same time, without a common background with his fellows he will be alien and adrift in the world. Interest and skill in one's work, whether it be making automobiles or teaching Greek, an acquaintance with the contemporary world, an alert intelligence which is always seeking to diminish the area of things human that are alien to one—a man or woman with this would be truly educated in any society. But both focus and background are supremely necessary. The present educational system does not really set itself to provide either. Only in a school organized on some such plan as the Gary plan will such education be possible.

This does not mean that every child is to marvelously blossom into ideally alert and skilled intelligence. But we can be sure that a school which gives opportunity for the development of the most varied aptitudes in the free play of a child-community life will have done all that it could. No one pretends that the Gary education is the intrinsically ideal education for all time. But we can say that, given the best social demands of America to-day, this school will make for the most robust, effective, intelligent citizenship of which we are at present capable.

XIX

THE TRAINED MIND

How much longer are we to expect the headmasters of our private secondary schools to view with anything but alarm the current radical tendencies in education? In the November "Atlantic," Dr. Alfred E. Stearns of Phillips-Andover is stirred to wrath against the fallacies of the modern school as expounded by Mr. Flexner and others. The paper contributes little new to the well-worn theory of mental discipline upon which upper-class education has so long been based. But it is highly significant as a pattern of the "trained" mind as it works in the exposure of fallacies. Dr. Stearns is presumably an immensely successful product of the old idealistic and linguistic education, gained by strenuous effort and vigorous thinking. It is worth while to examine how such a mind argues, what it considers as clinching evidence, how it hopes to convince the alert intellectual of to-day.

The "fallacies" in modern education which Dr. Stearns is exposing are the materialistic and utilitarian ideal, the belief in the non-transferability of mental power from one field to another, the cultivation of interest rather than discipline, of play rather than drudgery, the scientific rather than the cultural emphasis. He wishes to persuade the reader that all these tendencies make for the perversion of the child's character, the weakening of his mental grasp, the materializing of his soul. One waits eagerly for proofs of such very serious menaces. The student of education to-day is rapidly acquiring a belief in objective evidence, in statistical or at least analytic experiment, in scientific formulation. The kind of evidence that appeals to the alert student to-day is the kind that comes out of the psychological laboratory of Clark University, or Columbia or Chicago, out of the great city school surveys, like Portland or Cleveland or New York, out of the experimental schools in different parts of the country. These are the arenas where educational problems will, he believes, ultimately be solved. And to him the so-called "fallacies" in modern education are not "dogmas" or "assumptions" at all, but rather hopeful hypotheses which are now being tested in dozens of American schools.

Is this the sort of evidence to which Dr. Stearns' trained mind appeals when he wishes to discredit the "new" education? Not at all. He does not even so much as show that he is acquainted with the existence of the great mass of literature which would throw light on the success or failure of the radical theories which he deplores. Educational journals, school surveys, reports of intelligence tests, descriptions of play schools,—none of these seem to have come into contact with his training. For the benefit of the philosophically-minded, he does not even refer to the writings of Dewey or Hall, or the other radical writers on education. All this writing and doing which represents the new education at work, he lumps into "the pedagogical expert," upon whom he lavishes his anxious scorn. The only concrete data he offers is the record of the College Examination Board, which Dr. Flexner, whom he is criticizing, had cited in his "Modern School." Dr. Flexner had argued against Latin and mathematics in the secondary school on the ground that the majority of even the picked students failed in them. Dr. Stearns succeeds in showing that a majority of college candidates fail not only in Latin and Algebra but in all other subjects as well. The normal mind, untrained by the old dispensation, would consider these statistics very damaging to Dr. Stearns' cause. The inexorable conclusion would be not that Latin and algebra should be retained in the secondary school curriculum, but that the entire curriculum should undergo a radical reorganization in teaching methods and educational philosophy.

Dr. Stearns, like most of the critics of the "new" education, makes the fundamental error of confusing the narrow business man, who sees no "use" for his son's taking Latin or algebra in school, with the "new" educator who would give these subjects a new orientation in the curriculum. The "practical" business man is as much anathema to the "modern school" as he is to the cultural school. The "modern school" would not refuse any subject to minds that fed upon it and fused it into vital experience. But it would not force it on minds that could not digest it. And Dr. Stearns' own figures show how generally indigestible, with all the drudgery and mental discipline in the world, is the entire conventional secondary school curriculum. The pseudo-modern high school where science and manual arts have been added, only to be taught in the same unilluminated way, is as objectionable to the "new" educator as it is to Dr. Stearns.

Since the latter's only use of objective evidence proves a boomerang, what considerations does he think will be persuasive in his attack on the "new" education? It is easy to see. His reliance is entirely on authority, upon personal belief. Several very successful business men of his acquaintance attribute their success to the training of the old education. The majority of schoolmasters are not yet ready to abandon the doctrine of mental discipline. The sons of Mr. Hill go to college to get something which their father, for all his success, recognizes that he missed. It is a serious question in the minds of many observers whether Dr. Eliot's advocacy of "observational" training is sound. Always the reference to personal authority, to prestige, to anything but objective standards on which both sides may agree! Always the naïve appeal to schoolmasters and successful business men, the pillars of his world! Dr. Stearns deplores the materialistic trend of the age, but he does not consider how powerfully his own innocent use of the verdict of successful business men as scientific evidence is likely to glorify material success in the minds of his students.

Dr. Stearns' logic is as unconvincing as his evidence. A doctrine is monstrous. Therefore, he implies, it is untrue. Intelligent children are usually bright in all their school subjects. Therefore, if you force a child to learn through drudgery, you automatically endow him with general intelligence. The interest of boys in wireless telegraphy and automobiles, he thinks, is the best argument for keeping all these things out of a school where one must learn to work. At the same time, Dr. Stearns objects to scientific schools because students so soon lose interest in their work. But, according to the gospel of drudgery, why would not this make science the ideal "mental discipline"?

Such a paper as this shows the technique of a thoroughly obsolete mind. Such "mental discipline" as this old education gave is evidently of little use in handling a world of facts, of experiment, of recorded tests. Criticism does not make such thinkers critical. It only makes them belligerent. They do not analyze, they repel. They are more interested in a moral justification for the structure of their craft and their practices than in the truth. Dr. Stearns' paper is the best evidence of how little relevant is the old linguistic and idealistic education to the intellectual demands of to-day. The critical, analytic, impersonal, experimental approach is wholly lacking in his paper. His evidence is personal authority, his logic is special pleading. Parents with sons in private schools might well view with grave concern the kind of "trained mind" which is likely to be developed under such masters of the old education. They might ask how likely a boy, taught to use his mind the way Dr. Stearns uses his, is to analyze and grasp the complex facts of the world into which he will come.

XX

CLASS AND SCHOOL

The proposed experimental school which the General Education Board is to found in conjunction with Teachers' College in New York has sent a shiver through the conservative schoolmen of America. It is assumed that the policy of the new school will follow Dr. Flexner's manifesto of the "Modern School," that adroit and uncompromising crystallization of the radical philosophy of our new American education. Dr. Flexner has proved himself to be an admirable agitator, for he has succeeded, with doctrines that public-school educators have been discussing for ten years and which experimental schools all through the country have been testing out, in rousing the slumberous camp of private secondary schoolmasters to a sense of what is going on in the educational world. The private secondary school is the last stronghold of educational conservatism. Enlightenment has to proceed upward through thick layers of prejudice and smugness. Dr. Flexner's voice seems to have broken in the walls and gotten a hearing for the new education even in the walls of the traditional New England academy. It is for these people that the "Modern School" was written, for only those will find its proposals "revolutionary and dangerous" who have never read a line of Dewey or G. Stanley Hall, never read a copy of an educational journal, never visited an experimental school, or even the newer plants of the best public schools in American cities. There is irony in the location of the new school at Teachers' College. For the latter has been one of the most persistently experimental educational centers in the country. If its "model" schools have felt in the course of time the blighting touch of conventionality, at least in the Speyer course of industrial arts there has been developed a method of permanent value. There is no more accurate application of Dr. Flexner's demand that "children should begin by getting acquainted with objects," "follow the life-cycles of plants and animals," "the observation and execution of industrial and commercial processes," and so forth. In this industrial arts course the children are concerned from the beginning with food-products and clothing and building and the way different peoples make their living. Out of this handling of homely things grow the geography and science and history and mathematics. It seems only a question of time before there will be scarcely an elementary school untouched by this practical approach to knowledge through objects and projects and concrete facts.

Dr. Flexner's tilting is not against our rapidly improving public elementary school so much as it is against the private secondary school, with its sub-college, classical, formal curriculum, and its obsolete educational theory of formal discipline and salvation through drudgery. It is as an object-lesson for this branch of American education that the new school will have permanent value. It will be the heaviest assault which has yet had to be met by that vested educational interest which we know as the private secondary school. The private school has made it its function to prepare the sons and daughters of the well-to-do for college, and so keep up the tradition of leisured and cultured wealth. This is the ideal at the bottom of the hearts of the conservative schoolmen. A knowledge which is useless, like the formal classics and mathematics, is only a sharpened tool of exclusiveness, for only the younger generation of a ruling class can afford to give its time to it. In a growing industrial society such an education becomes ever more and more a dividing line between classes. That the public high school has been largely controlled by the same ideals does not mean at all that this kind of education has been democratized, but merely that the unthinking and clambering middle classes have been hypnotized by vague aspirations of "culture" and "intellectual training" into imitation of the traditional ruling-class education. Some of the strongest opposition to vocational education in the public schools comes even from the ranks of the ambitious wage-earners who "want their children to have the educational advantages they were denied." They resent what they misinterpret as an attempt to keep their younger generation in a subordinate labor class. What they do not see is that the traditional education which they admire is no real education for the modern world. We find the industrious proletarian and the exclusive Tory joining hands in opposing the new democratic education which is meant to have the effects of freeing both classes and making them fit together to administer a free society. The Tory wants to keep for his children his privileged status; the wage-earner wants to obtain for his children this privileged status. "Book" education, innocent of practicality and use, is still an accepted mark of this geniality. Neither class has any real sense yet of a democratic attitude that finds both the "utilitarian" and the "cultural" irrelevant terms, and demands only effective activity and imaginative understanding from every citizen up to the limit of his capacity.

The "old" education then is a class-education, and therefore has no place in a society which is trying to become democratic. How much class-feeling is behind the current allegiance to the education of discipline and drudgery is shown in a paper by Miss Edith Hamilton of the Bryn Mawr School in the "New Republic" for February 10, 1917. She pleads for the "old" education in behalf of her girls. But when she says "school" she has in the back of her mind an institution for the training of the well-to-do classes. Her argument against a change in education seems to be based on the idea that change would be prejudicial to the life which she accepts as worthiest for those fortunate classes with which she is best acquainted. Her argument is that life will make no stern demands upon the sheltered, economically endowed leisure which most of her girls will enjoy. Without external standards their fiber must deteriorate unless they have learned the joy of work by the doing of things because they are hard. Without impersonal intellectual interests, their personal energy, she says, will waste away in futility or in a meddlesome control of their own daughters. The boy is harnessed into some kind of self-discipline by the exigencies of business life. But for the girl, the substitution in the "modern school" of domestic science for "elegant accomplishments" is only an illusory discipline. Not only are these arts of housekeeping too easy to provide discipline, but they will never be demanded from the upper-class girl. Only the traditional curriculum, therefore, impersonal, cultural, laborious, will give her the needed stimulus to play her leisured rôle worthily.

At first sight nothing could be more ironic than this gospel of strenuous effort preached in the name of a sheltered class. Why should a girl be disciplined, trained to do things "*because* they are hard," for a life which becomes "easier and easier," unless her teachers wish to provide her with some kind of moral and intellectual justification for her social rôle? The "old" education combines uselessness and effort, and it is just this combination which would maintain leisure-class functions and yet leave the individuals morally justified. The uselessness makes you exclusive and the effort satisfies your moral sense. It is a little curious to find Miss Hamilton using the "utilitarian" argument against domestic science, that is, that it will never be used by her girls. Yet she wishes them to acquire "impersonal intellectual interests," which they can never use except in not very real "cultural" dabblings and social work.

Miss Hamilton's argument for tradition is the orthodox one that is now being repeated by all those who oppose the new Rockefeller school. "The old education is superior to any training which makes interest not discipline, efficiency not knowledge, the standard." Now this point at issue between interest and discipline has been so thoroughly discussed by John Dewey in his "Interest as Related to Will" and other writings, that one is surprised at this late day to find responsible educators who are willing to give the impression that they are unacquainted with Dewey's arguments. Even if disciples like Dr. Flexner and myself in our enthusiasm unconsciously caricature him, the philosophy is there in its classic form in Dewey for all to read. The curious notion of the "old" educator that interest makes work "easy," instead of intensifying the effort, is only possible, of course, to minds soaked in a Puritan tradition. Dewey shows that interest and discipline are not antagonistic to efficiency and knowledge, but that knowledge is merely information effectively used and manipulated, and discipline is willed and focused interest. Each has an element of the other. It is meaningless to talk of interest vs. discipline when all real interest has an organizing effect on one's activity, and any real discipline is built up on a foundation of interest. Indeed in one of my articles to which Miss Hamilton takes exception, I define discipline as "willed skill," which is as far from any conception of "making things easy," of "smattering and superficiality," as could well be imagined. It is a superstition, of course, as Miss Hamilton says, to suppose that all children burn with a hard gem-like flame of curiosity to know, but it is equally a superstition to suppose that with all children strenuous drudgery flowers into the immense joy of work and creation, or that effort taken consistently against the grain of interest can suddenly be transmuted into spontaneous activity. A certain habit, a mechanical routine spirit, may be evolved by drudgery, but not imaginative skill. All true discipline comes from overcoming obstacles beyond which one is conscious of a goal in itself worth while. It is only a feeble spirit which can be drugged by effort in and for itself. In those admired cases where facility comes after conscientious but uninteresting effort, let the old-fashioned educator ask herself whether the child gained the satisfaction of accomplishment *because* he went through the discipline, or whether it was not only *because* he liked the satisfaction of accomplishment that he was willing to go through the drudgery. If you admit the latter, then you have admitted the case for the new education. Temperaments, impulses, interests—or, if you like, the lack of interests—will insist on dominating, on determining the way each child takes his experience. All education can ever do is to provide the experience, and stimulate, guide, organize interests. Anything else may produce, at its best, a trained animal. It will not be education, and it will not produce men and women.

The task of the democratic school is to provide just this general experience and stimulation. Miss Hamilton's paper shows that such a school would be a challenge to the kind of institution she has in mind when she speaks of education. When leisure-class functions and leisure-class education clasp in a perfect circle, a new sociological and industrial emphasis, such as the "Modern School" suggests, might make the leisure-class pupils uneasy, restless, questioning. If you began emphasizing interest instead of drudgery, you might find yourself calling into question the sincerity of those "impersonal intellectual interests." If you emphasized efficiency instead of knowledge, you might make uncomfortably evident the unreality of much of what passes for culture in society to-day. You would be making insecure the moral and intellectual justifications of caste. But that is exactly the critical and undermining work which a democratic education is designed to stimulate.

These new educators are seeking a type of school which shall provide for children as human beings and not as members of any one social class. They want a school which creates a common sympathy, a common intimacy with the various activities and expressions of the modern well-rounded personality, just so far as each individual is capable, with his endowments and intelligence, of acquiring such an intimacy. The "Modern School" would turn the child's attention to the projects, objects, processes, facts, of the active world about him, not because they are good in themselves, but because they are the common stock of all classes. The development of communal functions and services forces every family more or less into touch with the active world out of which the "Modern School's" curriculum grows. It is in the study of these "real things," rather than in the logical systems of text-books, the predigested ideals of literature or a leisured class, the technical manipulation of dead languages and official science, that common interest and the sense of common possession will arise. The expectation is that interpretations and ideals which grow out of such a study will be more vital and sound because they will have come out of the child's own experience, and not have been merely shoveled into his memory. It is expected that the "strenuous effort" of the past, which was so much an effort of memory and routine, will become, in a curriculum harnessed to occupational life, an effort of interest and intelligent enthusiasm. Out of such a spirit and such a school should issue the self-sustained discipline by which all good work is done in the world.

XXI

A POLICY IN VOCATIONAL EDUCATION

Now that the passage of the Smith-Hughes bill is assured, interest moves to the distribution of this federal subsidy for vocational continuation and part-time schools. For the actual sums appropriated, even the maximum which will be available in nine years, are too small to be of constructive significance. Indeed there is something grotesque about the solemn and arduous study which went into the passage of this timid educational bill by a Congress which could appropriate a full third of a billion for armaments. The Smith-Hughes bill has all the aspect of a pious wish rather than the beginning of a thorough national policy in education. There was nothing revolutionary in this principle of federal aid. The principle was established by the Morrill act of 1862 and recently confirmed by the Smith-Lever bill for agricultural education. The halting character of this new legislation must be explained partly by the novelty of vocational training in America and by the extremely confused condition of mind about it.

We scarcely know yet how to institute a vocational education that will make out of our youth effective workers and at the same time free and initiating citizens. The hopeless lack of coördination between industry and our educational system blocks and bewilders our efforts. In working towards a solution we meet two very real perils. When we attempt a coördination we run the risk of turning the public school into a mere preparatory school for factory, store and workshop, producing helpless workers riveted by their very training to a rigid and arbitrary industrial life. The better trained they are, or at least the more intense their specialization, the greater will be their subjection. Organized labor fears, and not unjustly, that a public vocational education might be the means of over-crowding the labor market and thereby "furnishing strike-breakers to industry." This is always the danger when we attempt to adjust our training too tightly to existing industrial conditions. On the other hand, if we try to evade this danger and make the young worker's training more general, so that a number of fields of industrial opportunity will be open to him, we may leave him more helpless than ever, for he has no assurance of being fit for the very concrete demands of skill that paying industry will make upon him.

This is the dilemma. If the organization of vocational training is left in charge of the representatives of the employers, educators fear, and fear rightly, that the first result will ensue. If it is left exclusively in the hands of educators, the employers fear the other danger. Vocational education in this country has, therefore, run its uncertain course through experiments in continuation schools, "pre-vocational" courses in the regular schools, trade courses, "coöperative" courses, until a certain skepticism has been aroused in the minds of professional educators and the interested public whether we can institute a workable system at all in our present public school. Skepticism has meant hesitation. In spite of the propaganda and survey work of an influential society of educators, employers and labor men—the National Society for the Promotion of Industrial Education—progress has been very slow. Only eight states have provided for the encouragement of vocational education and in only one is continuation schooling compulsory. The whole movement has needed some very definite concentrated stimulus and some new, clear focusing of the issues.

This is the real value of the new federal bill. If it is negligible in its actual power for aid, its indirect effects should be of great importance in the way of stimulus. It will undoubtedly suggest to the majority of states the immediate establishment of a comprehensive system of continuation schools. The grants will be just large enough to make it seem possible. They are not nearly large enough to exempt the states from local appropriations. According to the federal bill these must duplicate the federal grants. The latter will therefore mean actual additional resources, an increment to local and state appropriations. If the states are wise, and appropriate this increment to the payment and training of teachers, then these small sums may be made to mean just the difference between the present hardly attained mediocrity of vocational teaching and a new and effective type of artisan-instructors.

The bill puts the distribution of the funds in the hands of such state boards as the legislatures shall designate. The latter may designate the regular state board of education, or a special board of industrial education working under the direction of the regular board, or it may create a new and independent board to handle these funds. No state is likely to trifle with this now thoroughly discredited "dual" system originally sponsored in Illinois under the form of separate boards controlled wholly by employing interests. The practical choice will lie between the purely "educational" control and the mixed educational, industrial and labor control, such as exists in Wisconsin. The objection to the former grows persistently on the ground that the new vocational methods and work tend infallibly in the hands of the professional educator to drift back to the academic. Educators have too often shown a willingness either to divorce the "pre-vocational" work entirely from the regular school, or else to emasculate it of its realistic potency. Instead of seeing the new practical emphasis infusing and reinvigorating the regular primary and secondary school, the enthusiast for the "new" education has too often had to watch merely the slow reduction of the vocational work to the old unimaginative level of "manual training." The question of control, therefore, which the new bill puts indirectly to the states is of the greatest moment, both to the traditional type of school and to the new activities. The board that distributes the funds will in the last analysis control the policy. Certainly the conservatism of the professional educator is far less to be feared than the narrowness and self-interest of employers' associations. In following the provisions of the federal bill that the aided schools shall be below college grade, for children over fourteen, the state board will control the standards of the individual schools. Whichever form of control is adopted, the trend towards state centralization of the school system is likely to be greatly strengthened.

In this development the states will be influenced largely by the experience of Wisconsin and Massachusetts, where the continuation schools, part-time schools, apprentice classes, which the bill encourages, have been longest in operation. The Wisconsin experience will be found particularly instructive. The state subsidizes its vocational schools by duplicating the funds raised by the community under an obligatory half-mill tax. The local schools are under the control of a special board of industrial education appointed by the local board of education, and consisting of the superintendent of schools with two labor representatives and two employers. The distribution of the state funds is in the hands of the regular state educational administration. There is an advisory industrial board of similar composition to the local boards. At present the situation is much confused owing to the reluctance of this state board of industrial education to remain merely advisory. A "developer" has been appointed as its secretary, an expert in the field, but without administrative power over the schools. His attempts at acceleration have produced their inevitable and intense resentment among the regular school officials. Obviously such a system, with two boards contending for mastery, creates an impossible situation. With the exception of this—and the actual effect of this very largely personal and political feud upon the local development seems to have been negligible—the Wisconsin system seems to be based on sound principles. The local industrial boards have worked with effectiveness and responsibility. In Milwaukee a remarkable system of continuation schools has been built up, which provides for no less than eight thousand children between the ages of fourteen and seventeen, children whom the public and parochial schools have sloughed off into "blind-alley" work, and at whose education and guidance the city makes a last stab in the four-hour-a-week continuation school. One definite principle these Milwaukee schools seem to have established—that education must not be "preparatory" to work, that there is no real place for the merely "pre-vocational," but that education should accompany work and do that just as long as there is anything to learn. The ideal vocational education will be a liberal "part-time" education, in which the school furnishes the background and the constant opening of new suggestions and possibilities, and the shop or trade or office provides the arena for acting skilfully on what is learned.

The Wisconsin system is particularly suggestive. For the local boards constitute one of our first American attempts at representation by interest instead of political parties or arbitrary geographical divisions. Their success is largely ascribed in Wisconsin to this fact, that they do accurately represent just the three classes most concerned in this form of education—organized labor, the employers, and the professional schoolman. The labor representatives are on the board to see that the policy does not swing over to narrow employing interests, the employers are on the board to see that the school is kept in touch with the practical demands of industry. The professional educator holds the balance of power between these two interests. With this administrative development to build on, with the improvement in teaching caliber that the new federal grants should bring, with the state centralization of the school system to which the new bill will give impetus, the future is good for a national system of education for work and with work, a free and democratic vocational training.

XXII

AN ISSUE IN VOCATIONAL EDUCATION

Nothing is more significant of the new spirit in public education than our use of the term "vocational training." It strikes out at a blow the old antithesis between the cultural and the utilitarian. For a genuine vocation implies neither a life devoted to thought, nor a dull mechanical job to which personal and artistic and intellectual interests are mere trimmings—recreations which can be easily omitted by those who cannot afford to pay for them. A vocation is rather a nucleus of any kind of interesting activity by which one earns one's living, and around which whatever else comes to one's experience clusters to enhance its value and interest. It is not fantastic to hope that the very demands of modern industrial technique will make of most trades just such nuclei. When we justify trade-schools and industrial courses by the existence of law and medical and engineering schools, we are implying that the skilled worker in modern industry can and should lead a life as genuinely "professional" as the lawyer and doctor and engineer.

New York City has at the present time (June, 1915) a unique opportunity to meet these important issues. In no other city has the question been so squarely presented. New York has to choose between what is called the Ettinger plan, put into operation by a local superintendent to solve "part-time" and vocational training problems, and the Gary plan, as worked out by William Wirt and now on trial under his personal direction in several of the New York schools. In that choice may be indicated the tendencies and purposes of industrial education in this country.

The Ettinger plan emphasizes in the sharpest way the difference between "cultural" and "industrial" work. The child chooses between them in his sixth or seventh year of school. If economic pressure is going to force him into manual work, he is allowed to try a number of different trades in the school industrial shops in order to discover what he is best fitted for. This hasty experimentation has received the schoolman's label of "prevocational." Having chosen his trade, the young worker specializes in the shop, under conditions as nearly as possible like the trade, continuing in trade-school or technical high school, or in the industry under a coöperative scheme, as in the German schools. His academic studies, as far as they are continued, are of a severely practical character, theory and science being used merely to explain the industrial processes which he is learning. The ideal is a specialized school, gradually breaking off from the traditional one and developing radically different methods and interests. The object of the industrial course is to turn out a competent workman who has escaped the blind occupations of those who leave school at the minimum age.

The school under this plan may give the child an elementary industrial training, with an intellectual orientation better than he could get under any system of apprenticeship, but it can scarcely be said to give a vocational training. The Ettinger plan treats the child solely as a potential workman who is to be absorbed as a permanent subordinate in one specialized trade of a rigidly organized industrial system. It makes of the school a mere downward extension of the staple trades and machine industries, a sort of kindergarten where the employer gets his workmen trained, free of cost to himself. It quite ignores any other rôles the young worker may be called upon to play in society—as citizen or as member of an economic class. It makes an undemocratic class-division in the public school, and by divorcing the academic from the industrial work gives to both the wrong setting.

The Gary plan, on the other hand, prepares for a genuinely vocational life. It views the world outside the school not as a collection of trades but as a community, a network of occupations and interests, of interweaving services, intellectual, administrative, manual. It sees the individual as a citizen who contributes his share to the community and pays for the things he enjoys. The school itself is organized as a community, self-supporting industrially and as varied in its work, study and play as is the larger community. The industrial work is made an indispensable part of the maintenance and enhancement of this school community life. The Gary child begins in his third or fourth school year as helper in a shop or laboratory that interests him. If he is to work at a trade after he leaves school, he gets a long and thorough training under real workmen in the school shops engaged in the repair and maintenance of the school-plant. He is at no time called upon to choose between the "academic" and the "industrial." His work is a focusing of all the interests of the school, and the attitudes developed in the school are bound to be carried into productive life and to give a new setting to the business of making a livelihood. Science, apart from the light it throws upon the artisan's trade, is bound to mean something to him, for in the Gary school it has answered his questions about the physical world around him. History and geography and sociology and economics are likely to mean something because they have answered questions about the social institutions and the relations of men. Art and music will continue to interest him because they have been an integral part of the school life. The Gary plan would tend to produce not only a skilled workman but a critical citizen, ready, like the energetic professional man, to affect the standards and endeavors of his profession and the community life.

The Ettinger plan is as economically unsound as it is pedagogically unsound. It requires special teachers, and expensive shops which are unproductive. Without state or federal subsidies, the cost of any extensive or even adequate industrial training in trade-school or elementary school will continue to be prohibitive. The Gary plan, which connects the school shops directly with the repair and maintenance of the school-plant, demands and can afford a much greater variety of shops than the ordinary school. And since the workmen-teachers earn their salaries by their work, the children get their industrial training practically without cost to the community. By the Gary plan the vocational training features are only practicable if all the other liberally varied "cultural" features are put into operation at the same time. This effectually prevents that "exploitation" of the children which its opponents fear because the young workers get their training as "apprentices" in the school shops.

Many who admit the superior social aims of the Gary plan are inclined to feel that the practical results of the two plans will not be radically different. But the Gary plan and the Ettinger plan are not merely two different ways of reaching the same end. They not only involve different conceptions of the school and of industrial society, but they are bound to turn out different kinds of people.

The Ettinger plan is dangerous because it is typical of most schemes now being put forward by the advocates of industrial education. These plans are concerned neither with genuine educational interests nor with genuine industrial interests, but only with the interest of the employer. No person who feels that the public schools should train critical citizens who will have something to say to the industrial system into which they go, and not mere docile workers, counting socially no more than their tools, will fail to realize the vast importance that the Gary plan should prevail over all these schemes.

XXIII

ORGANIZED LABOR ON EDUCATION

At a recent labor conference in New York City, May, 1916, called to present a program for the local public schools, Mr. Gompers expressed himself as open-minded towards the Gary plan which is about to be extended to thirty-five more New York schools. This open-mindedness of Mr. Gompers is in welcome and significant contrast to the attitude taken by some of the smaller leaders in the city, who have apparently tried to line up organized labor with a personal political machine and with reactionary schoolmen in obstructing the reorganization of the elementary schools. But organized labor has better business than opposing educational reform, and Mr. Gompers's remarks, made with full responsibility and in direct opposition to the thinly-veiled partisan spirit of the conference, suggest that the responsible leaders of labor are willing to take a more enlightened stand in this important movement.

Organized labor has repeatedly gone on record in favor of a public school system which will train a labor citizenry so versatile and intelligent as to be able to protect itself from exploitation and the hazards of our social shiftlessness. It has demanded that vocational teaching be kept intimately related to life, so that children come out from the school neither helpless unskilled workers nor narrow machine-tenders, but potential citizens acquainted with the backgrounds of their crafts, with the significance of the labor movement and the institutions and movements of the world about them. Labor above all classes has a vital interest in an education for all children which acknowledges the full intellectual and social meanings of industrial processes and occupations. The education that labor desires is one which will give, particularly to those who engage in industrial callings, the desire and ability to share in social control, and to become masters of their industrial fate.

Now organized labor must be rapidly coming to see that this demand will never be satisfied by the conventional type of city public school. A traditional school founded on the bookish education of a leisure class can never be made into a pre-vocational school that will give power and dignity to labor, without a fundamental transformation of the present spirit, subject matter and teaching methods. An elementary school which gives its children no more than narrow drill in the three R's plus a little remote and unreal text-book information in history and geography, with what little half-hearted music and drawing and nature-study can be squeezed in, will never provide the foundation that the trained worker will need. No system of trade-training or vocational education superimposed upon such an elementary school will remedy the evils. Children who have been listlessly and ineffectively drilled in book-work will have acquired attitudes that are likely to be carried over into vocational work. Except for the few, industrial training will seem sheer drudgery, for it will have its roots in no interests and powers developed in earlier years. Pre-vocational education must mean something more than a mere sop to the motor-minded boys and girls who are restless with their books and are on the verge of leaving school for work. Such training, if it is to mean anything, must be woven in as an organic part of the school course. The entire elementary school could be a general, free, spontaneous, amateur pre-vocational school, where in direct contact with machines and industrial processes as well as books, with gardens and gymnasiums as well as laboratories and kitchens, with tools and print and pottery shops and drawing and music studios, children might have their imaginations stirred, try out their busy hands on things, and gradually sift out of the variety the interests that they can lay hold on with some promise of creative use. The school might be a place where play passed insensibly into work, and aimless experiment into purposeful construction.

Most of the current criticism of the public schools arises from the rapidly growing conviction that only in such a school will the modern city child have a chance to be educated in any way which will meet the demands in industrial or commercial life that will be made upon him. There is danger in current educational experiments that we become too easily satisfied with the mere addition of desirable courses, without at the same time transforming the school so that the new work is organically assimilated. Labor cannot be content with the school reform which many cities are adopting in the introduction of vocational courses merely in the upper grades. Such a postponement means an invidious class-distinction in those grades between the children who are going on to academic work and those who are going on to industrial work. It broadens the gulf between labor and leisure rather than diminishes it. Labor should be the first to protest against these "pre-vocational courses," "junior high school plans," as they are variously called. A school which consists merely of six years of bookish schooling with trade-learning and athletics tacked on at the top would merely intensify the evils under which labor now suffers. It would produce mechanical drudges. It would almost guarantee that industrially exploitable horde of young workers the creation of which organized labor so much fears.

In advocating such a system the lesser labor chiefs in New York have been very badly advised. The program of "immediate demands," put forth under Mr. Gompers's nose with a great flourish of the rights of labor, is not only unprogressive but actually reactionary. It is exactly the kind of specious program that the narrow-minded employer might demand who wished a docile but intelligent labor force trained at the public expense. In whose interest does labor demand the "immediate elimination from the course of study of any activity which takes away from the essentials and fundamentals of education in the elementary schools?" To eliminate organized play, auditorium dramatics, shopwork, gardening, dancing, etc., is surely the best way to drive children out of school, or to train them into mere appendages to machines. What labor needs is the most varied kind of work-study-and-play school, where imagination and interest are awakened. Yet here we find a conference on organized labor and education demanding simply more of the old kind of traditional schools! What good will it do to have more school buildings, more teachers, more pay for teachers, even more night-schools and playgrounds, if the schools merely pursue the old limited grind? Labor needs a school enriched in opportunity and vitalized with the modern spirit of "learning by doing," yet all it can think of to demand is "a seat for every child"! And to ram home to the public a sense of its straitened vision, this conference records its "emphatic protest against any further extension of the Gary plan."

Now opposition to the Gary plan may be a useful attitude for the lesser labor leaders who are playing for political stakes, but we cannot believe that this is the attitude of the intelligent elements in the labor movement. For what the Gary plan does is exactly to make possible for the first time on a large public scale this greatly enriched elementary school which labor needs for the realization of its own expressed educational ideals. The broad curriculum, the flexibility which adapts the school to the needs of every child, the interweaving work, study and play, transform the traditional school into a kind of child-community, where children throughout the course are laying the rudiments of their vocations. They have a chance from the early years, by trial and error, by experiment and realization, to find out what they can do and what they cannot do. To quote Superintendent Wirt, the Gary school is educating them just as the home, shop and school teacher educated the children of earlier American days. No formal pre-vocational course begun in the seventh or eighth year can do what this simple intimate contact with things and processes does. In a sense, industrial education may begin in the Gary school as soon as the small child is interested in going into the school-shops or laboratories as helper or observer. All the activities may be tested in the same way. The school is thoroughly democratic because the opportunities, bookish, manual, artistic, are open on equal terms to all the children. For labor to oppose the Gary plan means that labor is suicidally opposing the very kind of school that holds out the most opportunity for an enriched education for its children.

Mr. Gompers and the other responsible leaders of organized labor could do nothing more important than make an immediate and thorough study of the educational promise of the Gary school. If organized labor were to put itself enthusiastically behind the Gary plan, it would have at once an enlightened policy on elementary education which would effectively prevent any insidious exploitation of the movement. It would be well if the responsible leaders would repudiate these lesser labor chiefs who manipulate education for political purposes. The time has come for a bold and progressive stand.

XXIV
EDUCATION FOR WORK

The urgency of vocational education in this country has been immensely reinforced during the past few years by the rapidly growing social solicitude for child welfare. Child-labor laws, compulsory education, minimum wage, children's courts, welfare bureaus, devised primarily as mere protective agencies for the weaker and less self-defensible members of the community, are now suddenly seen to involve a host of positive social responsibilities. We are recognizing that the state has a duty not only to save the younger generation from exploitation, premature labor and demoralizing environments, but also to give it every possible opportunity to be trained for an effective vocation. In particular, the recent raising of the age limit for child labor in many of the states, by keeping in school thousands of children who would otherwise have passed out to work, has put a great strain upon the public school. The challenge so far has done little else than make evident an alarming inadequacy of the present type of school to train children for the work which they will shortly be called upon to do. The school systems of the large northern cities are having thrust upon them great numbers of children for whose education, in this new sense of the word, they are unprepared. And the burden and urgency is one that will increase rather than diminish.

This is one of the lessons of a document like the recent admirable report of the Minneapolis Survey for Vocational Education, made last year under the auspices of the National Society for the Promotion of Industrial Education. It would be difficult to advise reading more important for educator, employer and employee than this cross-section of the skilled-labor life of a great American city, looked at with a view to vocational guidance. In Minneapolis all the conditions were at their best for such a social laboratory experiment. The rapid growth of manufacturing and the unusually high proportion of skilled industries make the demand for the training of workers paramount. The stringent state laws require attendance at the school until the age of sixteen or the completion of the entire elementary course. The city has a school system of high traditional excellence. Clearly all the factors that would stimulate a campaign for vocational education are here in their most exacting form.

The analysis here given of the training which the manufacturing and mechanical industries require for their various skilled positions, the training which public schools and special schools are purporting to give, the increase in resources which school and shop will have to make to meet the social demands made upon them—all this will be found typical in greater or less degree throughout the country. The most general impression one gets from the Survey is of industrial unpreparedness. The public school is seen not with its usual fault as an institution of general education which has ignored pre-vocational needs, but as a pre-vocational school of narrow and exclusive type, for the vocational training of the classes in the community whose actual need was least. For above the earlier years of rudimentary schooling there has been superimposed a bookish school which is really a pre-vocational school for the professions or for domestic leisure. The boys and girls whose futures were to be professional and domestic had the benefit of the public school. The vast majority, the motor-minded and those whose aptitudes were not intellectual, very properly and automatically left this bookish school as soon as they had obtained their rudimentary general education. When the state suddenly refuses to allow these children to leave the school until they have finished the elementary course, the school system is faced with the necessity of broadening itself from a narrow pre-vocational school for the professions into a pre-vocational school for all the industries and arts of the modern community. The smatterings of wood-working and domestic science which the city schools have introduced are shown not to have broadened the school in the least. Even the technical courses in the high schools have quite failed to meet the problem. Of the recent graduates from these courses in the Minneapolis schools it is shown that one-half went directly to college, only one-tenth passing into occupations for which the course could in any way be regarded as preparatory. Most of these students, moreover, went into drafting rooms. It may be said therefore that to the training of the great artisan class of such a modern and progressive city the public schools have contributed practically nothing. A typically American progressive school system with all its technical and manual accessories is shown functioning at its very highest limit as a pre-vocational school, not for skilled labor, but for the professions and what the Survey suggestively calls the "commissioned officers of industry."

The industries themselves, however, are found to be no more adequately engaged than the school in training their own workers. Apprenticeship has all but died out, and among neither employers nor employees is there any enthusiasm for its return. Yet, although all the trades require a constant supply of trained workers, no substitute has yet been found for apprenticeship. The movement for industrial education has at times seemed like an attempt of employers to get their skilled workers trained at public expense. The effort to establish separate boards in the cities for industrial education threatened to limit such training to the narrow skill which each industry would demand and to supply employers with apprentices at no cost to the industry itself. Fortunately the Minneapolis Survey warns against this narrow and sinister conception of vocational education. Industrial interests cannot shirk the responsibility for the special training of their workers. The rapid growth of "corporation schools" shows that at least the most prosperous and highly skilled shops and factories are accepting this responsibility. All the employer has a right to demand is that the school give the young worker a general pre-vocational training which will introduce him to the special trade work. The graduate of the elementary school should have been through a well rounded course which not only cultivated a general intelligence, but discovered, by submitting him to many different kinds of activity, his particular flair or knack, and thus enlisted his interest in further training for a particular vocation.

The elementary school should, in other words, be a general pre-vocational school, where the boy or girl could get a bearing towards every type of vocation. The Survey strikingly confirms the far-sighted vision of William Wirt and his unspecialized and varied Gary school in which the children from their earliest years are testing out their powers in shop and foundry and laboratory and studio and classroom. "What is needed," it says, "is not a course in special woodworking—the extent of manual work in most elementary schools of the present time—but rather organized training in practical arts which will include a variety of experiences fundamental to the life of the community. Woodwork, metal work, printing and bookbinding, clay modeling, concrete and electrical work, are some of the industries which give an opportunity for experience in certain fundamental processes which are most valuable to boys without respect to the occupation in which they may later engage."

In the last year of the elementary school, or in the years of the junior high school, more specialized technical courses could be introduced. For the advanced work, more and more responsibility should be thrown on the shop, the school providing the background of theory, the shop the practical application, and the student alternating between shop and school as in the so-called coöperative course. For the workers already engaged, part-time continuation classes are advised, with "dull-season classes," and evening trade-extension courses. For these the various special schools in the city, commercial and technical, could coöperate. In this correlation of shop and school a new form of apprenticeship would grow up. The Survey reports trade agreements already worked out in several trades which provide that after two years of high-school instruction in practical, technical and academic subjects, the worker will be placed in the occupation at wages equal to those of a third-year apprentice. The agreements require the approval of the union, and the employers agree to use the school as the first source of supply in engaging new workers.

On some such constructive lines as are suggested in this Minneapolis Survey will the problems of vocational education be worked out. In its discussion of such topics as home gardening, office work, art education, domestic service, the Survey suggests the breadth of the field to be covered. An ideal system of vocational training would not only give every boy and girl in the school an opportunity to find an aptitude and cultivate some skill but it would make possible the training of "non-commissioned officers" in the industrial army. The education of such leaders will really be the goal of organized vocational education. As the industries, trades and occupations become more technical and more scientifically managed, the demand for administrative, supervisory, directive and planning officers taken from the ranks is constantly widening. Efficient management is becoming recognized as almost the most important factor in production, and management will be the reward for intelligence and skill. Until we have an educational system which in coöperation with shop and factory gives fullest opportunities for each child in the schools to work towards qualifying as such a "non-commissioned officer" in some occupation of the social army, we shall not have our democratic school or our framework for the future democratization of industry. Nor shall we be able to attack those mountainous problems of unskilled labor which no system of vocational training can touch.

XXV

CONTINUATION SCHOOLS

The movement for vocational education has done nothing more valuable than to show us how far we are still from realizing the public school as a child-community, first of all as a quickening life and only secondarily as an educational institution. The rapidly extending "continuation school" is perhaps the most obvious symptom of this failure. The term itself is unfortunate, for it drags along with it the old separation of education from living. It suggests something in the way of a surplus, of extension schooling beyond an allotted time, as if its pupils were getting an educational largess out of some great social bounty. Actually the "continuation school" represents educational deficit; the necessity for it registers our failure to provide an earlier school-community life for children which would have kept them out of industry. Also it registers our failure to provide child-labor laws which would have protected them.

The continuation school is officially a "school for employed minors fourteen to sixteen years of age," and is intended to hold, by the tenuous thread of four to six hours a week school attendance, those boys and girls who have gotten their employment certificates at the earliest legal age and are floundering about in low-paid occupations, mostly unskilled. New York City alone has 58,000 such children, fourteen and fifteen years of age, two-thirds of whom have never completed the elementary school. Stores, offices, shops, domestic service, messenger service absorb these boys and girls, untrained and unfocused, and the truly formidable burden is placed upon them of making their skilful way in the world. Popular tradition tries to make us glow with the belief that this world is a ladder up which virtue and industry will automatically ascend. But unfortunately the ladder of opportunity rarely reaches down so far. The lowest rung is beyond their reach. The gap between it and the ground is often too great even for initiative and character to bridge. The "employed minors fourteen to sixteen years of age" become the nucleus for that partly employed, sodden and anemic mass of drifters which drags down labor everywhere and clogs social progress.

The education which these children have had has in most cases barely fitted them to remain upright on the ground, not to speak of reaching for the ladder. The acquirement of literacy, a more or less uncertain skill in figuring, the exposure to some miscellaneous historical and geographical information—this has been the real substance of their five or six years' schooling. To most of these children it is probable that the world of printed symbols will never mean very much. A real school would have striven to awaken their concrete and constructive intelligence, given play to all the non-intellectual impulses. It is just the tedium and artificiality of the old school which has sentenced them now to stand at the bottom of the occupational scale. Without class-prestige, economic advantages, manners, extraordinary initiative or intelligence, most of these children are handicapped from the start. Literate, they are perhaps fitted to compete on equal terms with each other for work. But for the passing into better-paid, more interesting, more responsible and skilful activity, their schooling, though it came at the most plastic and active time of childhood, has done nothing whatever.

We try, therefore, through the "continuation school" to make up bravely to these children what they have lost. We try to lift them so that they can clutch at the lowest rung of the ladder. We find it easier to make stabs at repairing the damage than to reorganize the elementary school so as to prevent it. In Wisconsin cities a boy or girl leaving school at fourteen to go to work is required to attend day continuation school four or five hours a week for three years. In Boston the children must attend for four hours a week for two years. In Pennsylvania cities they must attend eight hours a week for two years. Continuation schools for 20,000 children are in process of formation by the New York City Board of Education. Wisconsin's forty-five industrial and continuation schools are compulsory, while in the other states which have permissive laws the schools may be made locally compulsory. Employers are required to dismiss their child employees on working days and within working hours, the school time being reckoned as part of the time that minors are permitted by law to work.

Such laws obviously follow the line of least resistance. They add to the school system without revitalizing it. At the same time, a scheme like the Massachusetts plan suggests that the continuation school may be developed into a real stimulus of incentive. This plan provides for three kinds of classes. For those "employed minors" who are already in semi-skilled work, it provides some training and background for the trade or occupation chosen. There are also trade preparatory classes for pupils who have definitely chosen the trade for which they wish training, but have not yet found placement in the trade. Then there are "pre-vocational" classes for those who are ambitious to make some intelligent choice of an occupation. These pupils are given varied shopwork, visits to shops and factories, and personal consultation with teachers and employers. Classes are small, and intensive work can be done. The other pupils, employed in unskilled labor and without definite vocational leanings, go into "general improvement courses," where half the time is spent in regular school subjects continuing the elementary school work; a quarter of the time is devoted to "the discovery and development of dominant interests and powers," and the rest of the time to what is quaintly called "civics, hygiene, recreation and culture." In this latter activity one-quarter of the time of the "pre-vocational" and trade courses is similarly spent. Pupils may transfer from one class to another when they are ready. If the purpose of the continuation school is to bridge that gap between the ground and the level where opportunity can at all begin to mean anything, this Massachusetts plan would seem to do it in an easily graduated and flexible way. The untrained and unfocused worker has at least a chance to have his imagination stimulated and to learn the rudiments of some better work.

The sanguine advocates of the continuation school, however, are apt to assume that this chance is equivalent to an effective vocational training. They forget that of the 10,000 or more children whom Wisconsin provides with compulsory continuation schooling a majority must necessarily remain in the general improvement classes or else get only a rudimentary training. And five hours a week for education against fifty for routine labor is not likely to make over the boys and girls who are pulled into the school for a brief respite from the department stores, messenger and domestic service, mills and factories, millinery and dressmaking shops. Even in the stimulating Massachusetts atmosphere one hour a week for "civics, hygiene, recreation and culture" seems hardly availing. In the light of the kind of school-community life which every progressive state now knows enough to provide and could afford to provide, the continuation school seems a pathetic if necessary palliative for our educational sins. Already loud complaints are heard against "allowing the public school to pass on its failures for some one else to bury." The first lesson of the continuation school is that it should not be needed. Even employers repeatedly declare that to industry children under sixteen are of no real value as workers. The states are one after another jacking up their child-labor limit to sixteen years. We are rapidly coming to the public conviction that the school should care for all children's activity up to that age. What the continuation school does now for four hours a week, we are insisting that the regular school shall do for thirty or even forty hours a week.

But this means that we shall have to have a reinvigorated school. It must not be a prison where children are kept when they long for the freedom of outside work. It must be a place where full opportunity for expression is provided for each child in a varied life of study and work and play. It must be an organic life and not an institution. No system of industrial and continuation schools piled on at the top will effect this. The evening school has largely failed because it demanded an impossible concentration and perseverance from the over-fatigued and excitement-craving worker. The continuation school, dealing with restless and unintegrated children, will be ineffective for the same reason. The vocational movement goes blundering on in amazing disregard of the psychology of the worker. Even the docile German child, it is said, must be coerced into his admirable continuation school where he gets a thorough orientation in his relations to his work, the community and his comrades. What are admirable trades and studies going to mean to boys and girls who are doing the most rudimentary work, their impulses undirected, their minds filled with sex-fantasy, personal mirages, and all the cheap and feeble excitements of the city streets? The groping and desiring spirit of youth is going indomitably to resist your most thoughtful schemes until you have a school which from the earliest years, by its freedom, its expressive life, its broad communal and personal excitements, its contact with real things, provides a child-life which meets these inner needs. Our best American public schools already begin to show that such a child-community life is not at all impossible. Until we achieve it generally, our continuation school will be one of the stop-gaps, and a lusty warning of what we have failed to achieve.

XXVI

WHO OWNS THE UNIVERSITIES

The marked and immediate reaction of the thinking public to the Scott Nearing case shows a growing conviction that all is not well within the conventional forms of university control. It implies a sense that universities, whether supported by the state or privately, are becoming too vitally institutions of public service to be much longer directed on the plan of a private corporation. University trustees are generally men of affairs, and as men of affairs they naturally tend to hold the same attitude towards the university that they do to the other institutions—the churches and railroads and corporations—they may direct. The university officers whom they appoint seem to have exactly the same duties of upholding the credit of the institution, of securing funds to meet its pressing needs, of organizing the administrative machinery, which their corporation officers would have. Professors are engaged by contract as any highly-skilled superintendent would be engaged in a factory. If a well-paid subordinate of a mining corporation could not get along with his colleagues and his men, or if he consorted with the I. W. W. or made revolutionary speeches in the streets, his services would be dispensed with as readily as the Pennsylvania trustees rid themselves of the unpleasantness of Professor Nearing. Trustees may respect a professor more than they do intrinsically a fourth vice-president. They may tend to err, as Chancellor Day has suggested, on the side of "merciful consideration." But they cannot see that the amenities of the case materially alter the professor's status.

This would be the case of university trustees stated in its rawest terms. That they tend so often to act as if they were a mere board of directors of a private corporation gives rise to endless suspicion that they consult their own interests and the interests of the donors of the vested wealth they represent as trustees of the university, just as they would protect, as faithful corporation directors, the interests of the shareholders of the company. It is just this attitude which the thinking public is no longer inclined to tolerate. We are acquiring a new view of the place of the university in the community. When the American college was no more than an advanced boys' academy, there may have been some excuse for this form of control by self-perpetuating and irresponsible boards of trustees. But many things have changed since Harvard and Yale, Princeton, Pennsylvania and Columbia, were founded.

Now this determined autocracy may not have worked so badly when most of the trustees and practically all of the instructors were ministers of the Gospel, although even in those days faculties sometimes complained that their careful plans were overridden by men ignorant of collegiate business and little interested in educational policy. The demand that trustees' functions should be limited to the management of funds, leaving the faculties to regulate administration and control appointments is a hoary one. But with the passing of control from the ghostly to the moneyed element, the gulf between trustee and professor has become extreme. Professors have fallen into a more and more subordinate place, and the president, who used to be their representative, has now become almost entirely the executive agent of the trustees, far removed in power and purse and public distinction from the professor. The university president in this country has become a convenient symbol for autocratic power, but even when he has become a "mayor of the palace" and professors may not approach their governors except through him, the real autocracy still lies in the external board behind him.

This absentee and amateur form of university control is being constantly ratified by our American notions of democracy, and that folkway, which runs so omnipresently through our institutional life, of giving the plain ultimate citizen control, in order that we may be protected from the tyranny of the bureaucrat. The newer state universities are controlled in exactly the same spirit. Regents, elected by legislatures, have shown themselves quite as capable as the most private trustees of representing vested political interests. Nor has democracy been achieved by the cautious admission, in recent years, of alumni trustees, as in the case of Columbia, or, as in the case of Harvard and Yale, by the substitution of alumni for the former state officials. Self-perpetuating boards will always propagate their own kind, and even if alumni trustees were ever inclined to be anything but docile, their minority representation would always be ineffective for democracy.

The issues of the modern university are not those of private property but of public welfare. Irresponsible control by a board of amateur notables is no longer adequate for the effective scientific and sociological laboratories for the community that the universities are becoming. The protests in the most recent case imply a growing realization that a professor who has a dynamic and not a purely academic interest in social movements is an asset for the whole community. The latest controversy between trustee and professors seems to have been very definitely an issue between interested policy and accurate, technical fact. It seems to have been clearly a case of old tradition against new science, the prejudiced guesses of corporation officials against the data of a scientific student of economics. Any form of university control which gives the prejudiced guess the power over the scientific research is thus a direct blow at our own social knowledge and effectiveness. The public simply cannot afford to run this risk of having the steady forging ahead of social and economic research curtailed and hampered. We cannot afford to depend wholly on the tempering of trustees by the fear of the clamor of public opinion. It is wholly undesirable that trustees should be detained only by "merciful consideration" from discharging professors whom they find uncongenial or who they feel are spreading unsound doctrine. Make university trustees directors of a private corporation and you give them the traditional right of terminating contracts with their employees without giving reasons or any form of trial. But if the university is not to be a mere degree-manufactory, or a pre-vocational school representing the narrow interests of a specialized economic class, but is to be that public intellectual and scientific service that we all want it to be, the governance must be different from that of a mining company, and the status of the professor different from that of a railroad employee. Professors should have some security of office.

An interested public which feels this way will demand that the faculties be represented strongly in the determination of all university policy and in the selection and dismissal of the instructors. It may even demand that the community itself be represented. Trustees who really envisage the modern university as a public service, as a body of scientific and sociological experts, will gladly share their power. If they do not, they will demonstrate how radically their own conception of a university differs from the general one, and it will be the duty of professors to assert their rights by all those forms of collective organization whereby controlled classes from the beginning of time have made their desires effective.

XXVII
THE UNDERGRADUATE

In these days of academic self-analysis, the intellectual caliber of the American undergraduate finds few admirers or defenders. Professors speak resignedly of the poverty of his background and imagination. Even the undergraduate himself in college editorials confesses that the student soul vibrates reluctantly to the larger intellectual and social issues of the day. The absorption in petty gossip, sports, class politics, fraternity life, suggests that too many undergraduates regard their college in the light of a glorified preparatory school where the activities of their boyhood may be worked out on a grandiose scale. They do not act as if they thought of the college as a new intellectual society in which one acquired certain rather definite scientific and professional attitudes, and learned new interpretations which threw experience and information into new terms and new lights. The average undergraduate tends to meet studies like philosophy, psychology, economics, general history, with a frankly puzzled wonder. A whole new world seems to dawn upon him, in its setting and vocabulary alien to anything in his previous life. Every teacher knows this baffling resistance of the undergraduate mind.

It is not so much that the student resists facts and details. He will absorb trusts and labor unions, municipal government and direct primaries, the poems of Matthew Arnold, and James's theory of the emotions. There is no unkindliness of his mind towards fairly concrete material. What he is more or less impervious to is points-of-view, interpretations. He seems to lack philosophy. The college has to let too many undergraduates pass out into professional and business life, not only without the germ of a philosophy, but without any desire for an interpretative clue through the maze. In this respect the American undergraduate presents a distinct contrast to the European. For the latter does seem to get a certain intellectual setting for his ideas which makes him intelligible, and gives journalism and the ordinary expression of life a certain tang which we lack here. Few of our undergraduates get from the college any such intellectual impress.

The explanation is probably not that the student has no philosophy, but that he comes to college with an unconscious philosophy so tenacious that the four years of the college in its present technique can do little to disintegrate it. The cultural background of the well-to-do American home with its "nice" people, its sentimental fiction and popular music, its amiable religiosity and vague moral optimism, is far more alien to the stern secular realism of modern university teaching than most people are willing to admit. The college world would find itself less frustrated by the undergraduate's secret hostility if it would more frankly recognize what a challenge its own attitudes are to our homely American ways of thinking and feeling. Since the college has not felt this dramatic contrast, or at least has not felt a holy mission to assail our American mushiness of thought through the undergraduate, it has rather let the latter run away with the college.

It is a trite complaint that the undergraduate takes his extra-curricular activities more seriously than his studies. But he does this because his homely latent philosophy is essentially a sporting philosophy, the good old Anglo-Saxon conviction that life is essentially a game whose significance lies in terms of winning or losing. The passion of the American undergraduate for intercollegiate athletics is merely a symbol of a general interpretation for all the activities that come to his attention. If he is interested in politics, it is in election campaigns, in the contests of parties and personalities. His parades and cheerings are the encouragement of a racer for the goal. After election, his enthusiasm collapses. His spiritual energy goes into class politics, fraternity and club emulation, athletics, every activity which is translatable into terms of winning and losing. In Continental universities this energy would go rather into a turbulence for causes and ideas, a militant radicalism or even a more militant conservatism that would send Paris students out into the streets with a "Cail-laux as-sas-sin!" or tie up an Italian town for the sake of Italia Irredenta. Even the war, though it has called out a fund of anti-militarist sentiment in the American colleges, still tends to be spoken of in terms of an international sporting event. "Who will win?" is the question here.

Now this sporting philosophy by which the American undergraduate lives, and which he seems to bring with him from his home, may be a very good philosophy for an American. It is of the same stuff with our good-humored contempt for introspection, our dread of the "morbid," our dislike of conflicting issues and insoluble problems. The sporting attitude is a grateful and easy one. Issues are decided cleanly. No irritating fringes are left over. The game is won or lost. Analysis and speculation seem superfluous. The point is that such a philosophy is as different as possible from that which motivates the intellectual world of the modern college, with its searchings, its hypotheses and interpretations and revisions, its flexibility and openness of mind. In the scientific world of the instructor, things are not won or lost. His attitude is not a sporting one.

Yet the college has allowed some of these sporting attitudes to be imposed upon it. The undergraduates' gladiatorial contests proceed under faculty supervision and patronage. Alumni contribute their support to screwing up athletic competition to the highest semi-professional pitch. They lend their hallowing patronage to fraternity life and other college institutions which tend to emphasize social distinction. And the college administration, in contrast to the European scheme, has turned the college course into a sort of race with a prize at the goal. The degree has become a sort of honorific badge for all classes of society, and the colleges have been forced to give it this quasi-athletic setting and fix the elaborate rules of the game by which it may be won—rules which shall be easy enough to get all classes competing for it, and hard enough to make it a sufficient prize to keep them all in the race. An intricate system of points and courses and examinations sets the student working for marks and the completion of schedules rather than for a new orientation in important fields of human interest.

The undergraduate can scarcely be blamed for responding to a system which so strongly resembles his sports, or for bending his energies to playing the game right, rather than assimilating the intellectual background of his teachers. So strongly has this sporting technique been acquired by the college that even when the undergraduate lacks the sporting instinct and does become interested in ideas, he is apt to find that he has only drawn attention to his own precocity and won amused notice rather than respect. In spite of the desire of instructors to get themselves over to their students, in spite of a real effort to break down the "class-consciousness" of teacher and student, the gulf between their attitudes is too fundamental to be easily bridged. Unless it is bridged, however, the undergraduate is left in a sort of Peter Pan condition, looking back to his schoolboy life and carrying along his schoolboy interests with him, instead of anticipating his graduate or professional study or his active life. What should be an introduction to professional or business life in a world of urgent political and social issues, and the acquiring of intellectual tools with which to meet their demands, becomes a sort of sequestered retreat out of which to jump from boyhood into a badly-prepared middle age.

The college will not really get the undergraduate until it becomes more conscious of the contrast of its own philosophy with his sporting philosophy, and tackles his boyish Americanisms less mercifully, or until it makes college life less like that of an undergraduate country club, and more of an intellectual workshop where men and women in the fire of their youth, with conflicts and idealisms, questions and ambitions and desire for expression, come to serve an apprenticeship under the masters of the time.

XXVIII

MEDIEVALISM IN THE COLLEGES

If the American college is to have a part in that new educational movement which is beginning to make the school not merely a preparation for life but life itself, interested in what has meaning to the student at his particular age and situation, it will have to recast some of its most cherished practices and ideals. The large university to-day represents all stages in the adjustment of intellectual activity to social demands, from the intensely practical schools of engineering, correlating with the technical progress of industry, back to the departments of literary scholarship—perhaps as pure an anachronism as we have in the intellectual world to-day. The demands for technical knowledge have pulled the university along, as it were, by the nose, and strung it through the ages, so that a "professor" to-day may be an electrical expert fresh from Westinghouse, or an archaic delver into forgotten poetry.

The technical departments of the universities have kept bravely up with the work of "learning by doing." Laboratory and shopwork, practical coöperation with industry, contact with technical experts, have made the newer departments what they should be—energetic workshops where theory and practice constantly fertilize each other, and where the student comes out a competent technician in his craft. But the place of the college in this scheme becomes more and more anomalous. Devoted to the traditional studies—the literatures, mathematics, philosophy, history—it is still strangely reminiscent of old musty folkways of the schoolman and theologian. Every professor knows the desire of the average student to finish his college course and grapple with his professional studies. Every professor is aware of the sharp quickening of interest which comes on entrance to the professional schools. Though part of this feeling may be due to impatience to get out into the world, much of it certainly arises from a realization that at last one has come into a sphere where thinking means action. The college, with its light and unexacting labor, is cheerfully exchanged for the grind of the professional school, because the latter touches a real world.

Whereas the higher schools give the student active work to do, almost all the methods of the college teaching conspire to force him into an attitude of passivity. The lecture system is the most impressive example of this attitude, and the lecture system seems actually to get a tightening grip upon the modern college. As standard forms have become worked out, it is customary now actually to measure the student's course by the number of hours he exposes himself to lectures. For the college course to be organized on a basis of lectures suggests that nothing has happened since Abelard spoke in Paris to twelfth-century bookless men. It is as if the magic word had still to be communicated by word of mouth, like the poems of Homer of old. The emphasis is continually upon the oral presentation of material which the professor has often himself written in a text-book, or which could be conveyed with much greater exactness and fullness from books. These books the student knows only as "collateral reading." Nothing is left undone to impress him with the idea that the books and reviews and atlases are mere subsidiaries to the thin but precious trickle of the professor's voice.

Now there may be some excuse for the lecture in a Continental university, where the professor is a personality, is not compelled to lecture, and may make of his delivery a kind of intellectual ceremony. But American professors are not only likely to be atrocious lecturers, but to hate such compulsory talking as the sheerest drudgery. Too often their own palpable derision at the artificiality of it makes the lecture an effective barrier between the student's curiosity and its satisfaction. This is not to deny that the lecture might be made into a broad interpretative survey, which would give the student the clues he needs through the maze of books. This is exactly what the best college courses tend to become. But for this the college will need interpreters, and not the humdrum recorders and collators that it has a weakness for.

The continuance of the lecture system is only symptomatic of the refusal of the college to see clearly the changing ideals of scholarship. If the student has to think chiefly about exposing himself to the required numbers of lectures, and then to examinations which test his powers of receptivity, he will be forced into an attitude which we are discovering is the worst possible for any genuine learning. This passivity may have been all very well when education was looked upon as an amassing of the "symbols of learning," or the acquiring of invidious social distinction. The old college education was for a limited and homogeneous class. It presupposed social and intellectual backgrounds which the great majority of college students to-day do not possess. The idea of studying things "for their own sake," without utilitarian bearings, is seductive, but it implies a society where the ground had been prepared in childhood and youth through family and environmental influences. When higher education was confined almost entirely to a professional intellectual class, the youth was accustomed to see intellect in action around him. He did not come to college ignorant even of the very terms and setting of the philosophy and history and sociology studied there. Now, when all classes come to college, the college must give that active, positive background which in former generations was prepared for it outside. It must create the intellectual stomach as well as present the food.

We are learning that this can only be done by putting ideas to work, by treating the matter taught in the college as indispensable for any understanding or improvement of our modern world. In the technical schools, ideas and processes become immediately effective, but nothing in the college is really "used"; ideas are not put to work. Professors anxiously desire to "teach students to think," but they do not give them opportunities for that hard exercise which alone can produce trained thought. The college organs of expression, the debating clubs, literary magazines, newspapers, speaking contests, dramatic societies, etc., are usually amateurish, spasmodic, unreal. The flimsy background of the undergraduate is not to be wondered at where undergraduate expression in any channel is left by the college authorities unorganized and childish. And his low state must inevitably continue until ideas are not merely collected, with some vague idea of gilding the interior of his soul, but resolutely put to work. One reason for the overmastering devotion to athletics in the modern college is exactly its activity. In that field the student can do something. Here, thank God, he says, is a place where one can act!

To make intellectual expression and not receptivity the keynote of the college does not mean to turn it into an intellectual engineering school or to make it severely utilitarian. It should remain unspecialized, the field for working out a background for the contemporary social world. The paradox is that only by this practical exercise can any real cultural or scholarly power be attained. As long as the student can speak of "taking courses" the receptive and slightly medicinal character of college learning will be emphasized. Moreover, as the schools both above and below the college adjust themselves to the new conceptions of learning, the archaic forms of college will cause it to lag in the race. The reason for their persistence is, of course, that whereas the technical demands of industry and the keen emulation in the professions have sharpened the higher schools and forced a revision of ideals and methods, the practical application of the cultural studies of the college has not seemed so urgent. The turning of these cultural studies into power is to be the exact measure of our growing conviction that ideas and knowledge about social relations and human institutions are to count as urgently in our struggle with the future as any mathematical or mechanical formulas did in the development of our present.

9 789361 380853

Printed by Libri Plureos GmbH in Hamburg,
Germany